THE FLIPPED READING BLOCK

Making It Work

How to Flip Lessons, Blend in Technology, and Manage
Small Groups to Maximize Student Learning

Gina Pasisis

SCHOLASTIC

New York • Toronto • London • Auckland • Sydney
Mexico City • New Delhi • Hong Kong • Buenos Aires

Dedication

I dedicate this book to Jessica Dopka, an extraordinary teacher who inspired students to reach achievement levels that were nothing short of phenomenal. She did this by building a happy, respectful classroom climate in which self-directed learners, driven by purpose, were highly engaged and motivated. She expertly integrated technology, student reflection, and strategies for skill-building. Every time I entered her classroom, I saw magic happen. Her students adored her, and her colleagues looked to her as a teacher leader. She made more of an impact on the lives of others in her 28 years of life than most people could make in a hundred years.

Jessica Dopka

Acknowledgments

I have been privileged to be invited into many classrooms in which I have witnessed the joy of teaching and learning. Observing wonderful teachers, the world's greatest difference-makers, moved me to write this book. Thank you to all of those teachers who inspired me.

I am grateful to both Deborah Morgan and Debbie Lewis. They shared their delightful and wise students with me so that I could show The Flipped Reading Block strategies in action through photos and videos. Thank you to the students! It is because of students like you that I love teaching!

It would have been impossible to write this book without my editor, Joanna Davis-Swing, whose queries caused me to consider carefully every word in order to ensure that I communicate a clear and relevant message. I also greatly appreciate the visually appealing design created by Sarah Morrow.

Very, very special thanks go to the teachers who have the dedication to read this book as one of the many ways that they continually develop and perfect the art of teaching.

Finally, I am blessed to be supported and loved by my dear family, who served as my cheering squad throughout the writing of this book.

▶   ▶   ▶

Cover Designer: Jorge J. Namerow
Cover Photograph: Cathy Yeulet/123RF
Editor: Joanna Davis-Swing
Interior Designer: Sarah Morrow
Copyright © 2015 by Gina Pasisis
All rights reserved. Published by Scholastic Inc.
Printed in the U.S.A.
ISBN: 978-0-545-77345-4

1 2 3 4 5 6 7 8 9 10   40   22 21 20 19 18 17 16 15

Contents

Prologue

When I began teaching in the 1980s, I did not know my students very well because I did not hear their voices or ideas very often. Sure, I would call on a handful of students each class period, but most of the time they sat quietly in straight rows in chairs that may as well have been glued to the floor because they never moved. While they sat still and passively listened, I lectured. I learned quite a bit about the literature I read because I processed that literature daily through my monologues. It did not occur to me that I was the only one who was really learning and increasing in reading achievement.

Truly, I was no better than the teacher from the movie, *Ferris Bueller's Day Off*. Like that fictional teacher, I kept talking even when it was clear that I had lost my audience. Although I looked at my students and read their body language, slumped postures and droopy eyes, I did little to change my behavior. I just jumped around a little more and worked on adding as much drama as I could to my monologue. When I began to sing in vibrato, a few students awoke from their slumber with wide-eyed looks of surprise, but as soon as they realized that my monologue was going to continue, they slumped again, their heads fell to the side and, sometimes, their soft snoring could be heard despite my booming voice.

In my early years, I was one of many teachers who did not have a good understanding of how students learn best. Thankfully, brain research has brought us into an age of enlightenment! No mentor teacher of mine ever said, "You could try allowing students to talk to each other about what they are reading. You might even ask them to write about what they are reading and to share ideas with one another rather than having you as their sole audience." It was by sheer accident that I discovered that students are more engaged when they can communicate their unique ideas about text with each other. I had been talking to students about *Roll of Thunder, Hear My Cry* (Taylor, 1991) and expounding my views on the injustice created by racism when I was interrupted by the attendance clerk, annoyed at me because I had not submitted my attendance sheet on time. While I put my lecture on pause to look through my grade book and jog my memory about which students had missed each period, the students started talking with passion about their views on the topic. I looked around at my students transformed from zombies into animated learners who suddenly sparkled. In that moment, I decided to start teaching differently, with less focus on my voice and more focus on the voices of the students.

In the pages that follow, you will explore ideas for giving voice to readers through a flipped reading block. With the integration of technology into the reading classroom, teachers can allow all students to learn actively throughout a class period—*even* while the teacher works face-to-face with small groups. After all, it is only through active engagement with text that students increase their achievement.

Read on to learn how you can transform your classroom into an environment in which irresistible learning occurs from bell to bell.

Why Flipping and Blending the Reading Classroom Makes Sense

What Does "Flipped Classroom" Mean?

Within the traditional classroom community, students have done a great deal of listening while teachers, the sages and purveyors of information, have done most of the talking. After the confession and epiphany I shared in the Prologue, you can see that I admit my share of guilt, at least at the beginning of my career, of being an air-time thief. I deeply regret those years now that I understand the importance of students' actively processing information as they learn.

The desire to provide students with processing time in class has led some teachers toward a new strategy—the flipped classroom. In this teaching model, the teacher flips the traditional procedure of giving a lecture during class and homework activities to be done after class to assigning a lecture that is watched online at home before class, then having in-class activities based on the lecture.

Jonathan Bergmann and Aaron Sams (2012), known as fathers of the flipped classroom, describe how they discovered the benefits of flipping the classroom in *Flip Your Classroom: Reach Every Student in Every Class Every Day*. Weary from repeating lectures multiple times for absent students, these two chemistry teachers decided to create videos of their lectures. Although they recorded the videos for students who had been absent, other students learned that the lectures were online, and they began to watch them. The students liked online lectures because they could pause the video when they needed to process information and rewind the video when they wanted to listen to explanations multiple times. Some quick information processors could even speed up the video. Because of the unexpected positive response from students to the teacher-created videos, Mr. Bergmann and Mr. Sams began to move direct instruction from classroom lectures to recorded ones students viewed online. This opened up class time for engaging, active learning experiences and opportunities for the teacher to individualize instruction based on each student's needs.

The flipped model makes perfect sense in a reading classroom, too. Even though students benefit from using time in class to practice reading strategies while a teacher facilitates this process, the need for some explicit instruction from the teacher still exists. By using the flipped model, a reading teacher no longer needs to spend a large portion of the period lecturing but can instead utilize short bursts of direct instruction to have a powerful impact. Mini-lessons (with emphasis on the word "mini") provide students with opportunities to observe a teacher as he or she thinks aloud about text while reading it.

One of the benefits of recording these mini-lessons is that students can watch them over and over until they understand the strategies taught through the think-alouds. Stephanie Coleman (n.d.) theorizes that "spoken material in the classroom passes students due to a number of distractions, missed classes, tiredness, or boredom." In "Do You Know? Ten Things Everyone Should Know about K–12 Students' Views on Digital Learning," Project Tomorrow (2012) published the results of a survey of more than 350,000 K–12 students. These students expressed their views about online learning, and they reported the ability to learn at their own pace as the number one benefit of virtual learning.

In Chapter Two, you will learn ways to flip your mini-lessons so that students can watch and hear your explicit instruction online.

Putting lectures, screencasts, and other content online has become a growing movement, but doing so is not the critical piece of the flipped classroom. The beauty of the flipped classroom lies in what happens *during* class because the teacher no longer needs to gobble up the class minutes with the lecture. Because students can watch the lectures and mini-lessons on their own time, the teacher can design class experiences that allow students to get the most out of the time with the teacher and the other students. In this model, students learn the knowledge-based content by watching the video, and they can therefore explore the content at deeper levels during class with collaborative groups and a facilitating teacher. The teacher's time is freed up to personalize learning and work with small groups.

At Clintondale High School in Michigan, 52 percent of students failed English before the implementation of the flipped classroom. After teachers flipped their classrooms, the failure rate dropped to 19 percent (Green, 2012). Reading teachers with whom I have worked also found success with flipped mini-lessons about reading strategies.

Active Learning in the Classroom: A Blended Approach Including Both Online and Face-to-Face Experiences

Amazing advances in technology and immediate access to a worldwide web of information have left some educators wondering not whether the role of the teacher will change but rather whether the teacher will have a role at all. Take heart, my fellow educators, for while Google and YouTube can deliver information, these tools can never replace the teacher. The futuristic vision of holograms that instruct a school filled with eager learners who glide from one technological machine to another does not take into consideration that humans still find their greatest inspiration from other humans. The Internet may be able to provide information and answers quicker than any teacher, but today's learner still needs guidance in order to consume content with discrimination and make meaning out of complex text. It remains the job of the teacher to help students develop the necessary skills to evaluate the information they find online. Teachers are now, more than ever, a vital component in student learning because, while today's learners enter the classroom more well-informed than past generations, many struggle when they are asked to read and think critically. Teachers can design activities, both online and face-to-face, that will help students use critical thinking tools and develop their unique gifts.

This combination of online and face-to-face learning is often referred to as blended learning, a style of learning that has become increasingly common at universities and has become a rapidly growing movement in the K–12 world. While it might be appropriate at the college level to provide "blended" courses with less face-to-face learning time and more digital learning time, younger students need more time in the brick and mortar building. For one, they need to learn how to be contributing members of a community, and that happens best when students come to school each day and participate in a classroom community. Through active learning in a positive classroom community, students can increase specific skills. The Partnership for 21st Century Skills (2011) has identified collaboration, communication, critical thinking, and creativity as skills needed to be successful in a global world. Modern technology, with its myriad benefits, has created more opportunities for students to practice these skills, referred to as "The Four Cs." Because of this, online learning has become increasingly more popular, but I reiterate that students need *both* face-to-face and online communication. If we throw students into a purely digital world in which all communication happens through a device, we risk robbing them of important interpersonal skills. It is not uncommon for a young person, sitting next to another, to communicate by saying, "Dude, I just sent you at text." Rather than talking and communicating face-to-face, today's students post status updates, share photos, and tweet; and despite having thousands of online friends, some of the students I have encountered in the last decade have admitted feelings of anxiety in social situations outside of cyberspace. We want to protect students from falling prey to social ineptitude right at a time when working collaboratively, both online and face-to-face, is very important. More than ever, companies expect collective innovation from their employees.

Further, we are a society of dual working parents. It troubles me to think of students being left at home alone all day to work online. Our modern, tech-savvy students are capable of setting up their computers so that it appears they are writing on discussion boards and participating in web quests while they are actually on a "learning adventure" that adults have not designed. When I imagine a large group of Ferris Bueller clones, I leap from troubled to terrified.

With all of this in mind, I think it best that students participate in a carefully crafted blend of online and face-to-face learning within individual classrooms. After all, powerful learning experiences come from being a part of a classroom community. While Friedman (2005) may say the world is flat because everything we need is contained on a screen, humans cannot exist alone, with a computer as our sole companion. We still need to spend time interacting with each other offline. There is something about working face-to-face with another person that even video chatting cannot replace. The blended approach allows teachers to select the most beneficial elements of both online and face-to-face learning.

As we bring more technology into the classroom, some may falsely assume that our modern learners need, above all else, to be taught the latest technology skills. Certainly, teachers must allow students to manipulate technology, but technological skills alone will not prepare students for the future. Undoubtedly, today's iPad will be tomorrow's Big Chief Writing Tablet and number two pencil. With technology evolving at an alarming pace, we have no way of preparing students to operate future technological tools that have not yet been invented. Utilizing technology in the classroom should not occur merely for the sake of technology. Rather, it should be a tool to individualize learning as students reflect and make meaning out of content. Students can reflect on their learning and make meaning out of text when they participate in discussions on an online platform. Again, we still want to keep that face-to-face discussion piece in the learning process. In my own personal experience, as well as my observations of other classrooms, I have found that students engage in the richest face-to-face discussions

> In Chapter Five, you will learn how to develop an online discussion board that allows groups of students to reflect on reading strategies and process the meaning of text.

when they have a chance to quietly ponder on their ideas and organize their thoughts in writing first.

This is the idea that modern learners, whom Marc Prensky (2001) has dubbed "digital natives," already understand. I have witnessed these tech-loving young people in social situations during which they tweet and then talk about their tweets. A blended approach is the perfect solution to meeting the needs of the modern learner. Students use the online communication tools they love to help them prepare for the face-to face communication they need.

How Does Blended Learning Affect Student Achievement?

In today's high-stakes testing atmosphere, you may wonder what the research tells us about the impact of blended learning on test scores. The findings of a 2010 U.S. Department of Education report based on a meta-analysis of over 1,000 studies conducted in the previous decade showed that the differences in learning outcomes between purely online and purely face-to-face learning were minimal (Means, Toyama, Murphy, Bakia, & Jones). However, learning that was delivered through both online and face-to-face experiences had the greatest impact on student achievement. Yes, blended learning won the race.

Keep in mind that this meta-analysis was largely based on college students, since few studies had been conducted on the K–12 population at the time of the report. I think, though, that K–12 educators can still learn from these findings and transfer the discoveries to understand how to reach our younger students.

One study, for example, indicated that the purely online model resulted in higher levels of questioning and critical thinking (Tutti & Klien, 2008). Regardless of age, a learner has a better chance of retention if he or she thinks and questions. In a high-quality blended model, students post on discussion boards after exposure to content through reading or watching videos. Writing about what they have learned after exploring this content requires students to question and think.

Also, it is a well-established understanding among educators that engaged learners are successful and satisfied learners. The online component of a blended course offers students opportunities for metacognitive and active connections to the subject matter. When they engage in online discussions with peers and their teachers, they must examine their thoughts and find ways to make sense out of content through synthesis, analysis, and evaluation. During the face-to-face portion of the course, students can participate in collaborative learning, which is also highly engaging. A report by the National Survey of Student Engagement (2008) showed that blended coursework engages students more successfully than traditional coursework.

In addition to showing that blended learning has the greatest impact on student achievement over purely online and purely face-to-face models, the findings from the U.S. Department of Education report also illuminate which types of online learning yield the best results. According to the report, "effect sizes were larger for studies in which the online instruction was collaborative or instructor-directed" when compared to "studies where online learners worked independently" (Means et al., 2010, xv). The findings also show that "manipulations that trigger learner activity or learner reflection and self-monitoring of understanding are effective when students pursue online learning" (Means et al., 2010, xvi). With this information, any teacher who wants to implement technology as a tool for learning should ask, "Am I using this tool to increase learner activity, reflection, and self-monitoring of understanding?" If the answer is no, then the teacher should find another way to use the technology.

As more and more K–12 schools promote technology integration, we gather more data to support the blended model. A middle school in Coppell, Texas, has integrated technology in all classrooms. Teachers have employed the flipped classroom model and have all committed to the requirement that students must engage in online discussions about content. The teachers at this school have used discussion boards to trigger learner activity, reflection, and self-monitoring of understanding. Taking on this approach has yielded significant positive results. Before adopting this blended approach, 156 out of 902 students had failing grades. After implementing the approach, the number of failures dropped to nine (Dorhout, 2013).

> A teacher may ask, "How do I translate this research into best practices for a reading classroom?" Rather than focus on computer games for reading growth, we reading teachers should give students authentic text to read and interpret. Then, we should give students opportunities to reflect and collaborate on an online discussion board.

How Are Students Grouped During Active Classroom Learning Experiences?

In an active learning environment, students are no longer limited to whole-group instruction. Sometimes, the teacher guides while students work in partnerships. At other times, students work in small groups. While most teachers understand the importance of developing small groups within the classroom, the process of doing so can seem daunting. A reading teacher faces many conundrums: How do I decide how to group students when some research points to homogeneous ability grouping while other research shows the benefits of heterogeneous grouping? Do I guide groups of students through texts at their individualized levels or provide all students with the same text while offering higher degrees of support for struggling readers? Would my students benefit more from teacher-guided reading groups or student-directed book clubs?

No single approach meets every student's needs. Teachers must provide different kinds of instruction to reach different kinds of students. Likewise, a variety of approaches is necessary if a teacher wants students to accomplish a variety of objectives. This is why the word "blended" means more than just a mixture of online and face-to-face instruction. Flexible groupings—which are at times face-to-face, at times online, at times teacher-led, and at times student-led—allow you to tailor instruction to fit individual students and specific purposes. Throughout this book, you will see how you can combine modern, research-based best practices in reading instruction and use the online component to support these practices.

At this moment, you may already feel overwhelmed at the prospect of juggling online groups, face-to-face groups, teacher-led groups, and student-led groups. You might feel yourself moving nearer to what I, as a teacher, consider to be the dictionary's most terrifying word: *chaos*. To the rescue comes the word *blended* again, in a blended management system. You will realize how being as immovable as a stone and at the same time as fluid as the ocean will make your active learning environment run smoothly. In the style of a benevolent dictator, you will establish procedures that allow no flexibility in some areas while giving students freedom and choice in other areas. If you put into place some simple structures, students can move seamlessly from quiet reflection to energized discussion. I have observed many classrooms like this in action, and I have recorded the teacher behaviors that created this type of environment. I will share these teachers' secrets and their step-by-step procedures for creating structures that surround and support a thinking curriculum.

This type of classroom is well-suited to the digital native, who has grown up using a computer and multi-tasking. In this book, you will find ways to motivate contemporary learners by constructing an assortment of strategically planned tasks that will lead to reading improvement. We digital immigrants remember our linear-focused reading classes, during which we sat in one place and listened to a teacher's lecture about *her* reading experiences for an entire period. We exercised our long attention spans; that is for sure! It is natural for those of us who learned that way to have concerns about the cerebral price of jumping from activity to activity, but worry not! Baroness Susan Greenfield, a neuroscientist who has researched the effects of technology immersion on the brain, says that reading is the antidote to short attention spans (Freeman, 2012). Because of the importance of reading for the modern learner, I have included time for independent reading and partner reading in the flipped and blended reading block so that all readers can find success and pleasure in reading. Once students reach the enjoyment level, they begin to develop endurance for reading and are able to read for longer periods of time. Ironically, through the multi-tasking I encourage, your students could actually improve their attention spans along with their reading abilities.

The Traditional Reading Block vs. the Flipped Reading Block

In upcoming chapters, you will learn ways in which you might structure your flipped and blended reading block. Here is how the flipped reading classroom differs from a traditional approach:

Traditional Reading Block	Flipped Reading Block
DIRECT INSTRUCTION The teacher presents information to students in the classroom through lecture. Formative assessment occurs with: • teacher-directed questions aimed at individual students in a whole-class setting • pencil-and-paper quizzes and responses	**DIRECT INSTRUCTION** The teacher records a mini-lesson; students view it outside of class. Assessment occurs in a variety of ways, including: • online responses posted to a discussion board • entrance tickets that show the process of using a strategy (using an online chat tool or pencil and paper) • notes taken on mini-lesson *Chapter Two discusses how to design flipped lessons and effective formative assessments, both traditional and technology-based.*
GUIDED PRACTICE Students read "round robin" style from a basal or textbook as a whole group. Students discuss the text as a whole class.	**GUIDED PRACTICE** Students apply lessons from direct instruction with teacher scaffolding in: • partner activities as a follow-up to mini-lessons • strategy practice groups • book clubs *Chapters Three, Four, and Five share routines and strategies for setting up and managing partner work and collaborative groups, and strategically incorporating technology for accountability, engagement, and relevance.*
INDEPENDENT PRACTICE Students read independently and answer teacher-directed questions and write teacher-directed essays.	**INDEPENDENT PRACTICE** Students practice skills independently with: • daily in-class reading • responses on a discussion board • collaborative, student-designed projects *Chapters Five and Six demonstrate independent practice opportunities that capitalize on technology tools and student choice.*

Traditional Reading Block	Flipped Reading Block
ASSESSMENT AND GOAL SETTING The teacher sets goals for students, analyzes data, and assesses student progress toward goals.	**ASSESSMENT AND GOAL SETTING** Students set their own goals, analyze various forms of data, and reflect as they self-assess their academic and behavioral progress through: • rubrics • goal setting templates *Chapters Four, Five, Six, and Seven provide strategies for involving students in data-analysis, self-monitoring, and self-assessment.*
MOVEMENT Students sit in rows most of the time, and movement is limited.	**MOVEMENT** Students move from self-selected, independent learning spots to a variety of partner and small-group formations. The teacher intentionally plans for movement to occur during the class period. *Chapters Three, Seven, and Eight offer ideas for the intentional incorporation of movement in the classroom.*
CLASSROOM MANAGEMENT The teacher creates the rules and a one-size-fits-all set of consequences for breaking the rules. All procedures are teacher-directed.	**CLASSROOM MANAGEMENT** Students collaborate to create a set of classroom laws and norms for behavior. The teacher offers positive reinforcement to encourage behaviors that will lead to student success. When a student's behavior impedes learning, the student problem-solves to create a solution. The teacher's intervention is supportive instead of punitive. Students have jobs and responsibilities so that they feel they are an important part of a student-directed classroom community. *Management tips are woven throughout the book, and Chapter 8 specifically explores ideas for creating a positive classroom climate in which learners feel supported by the teacher and the other learners.*

You can see from this table how the flipped reading block allows for active learning and application of literacy skills with the teacher as a facilitator. A dynamic, modern reading classroom that leads to greater learning satisfaction and higher levels of achievement is within your reach. Read on for ideas!

Where Did I Get All of These Ideas?

I began teaching English and reading in 1986, and through my years as a teacher, I have learned what works and what doesn't. Most of my learning occurred by accident, usually because I made mistakes and had to explore ways to correct them.

Some of my ideas came from my own experiences, and you will read these stories throughout this book. Many of my ideas came from students. In addition to interviewing countless students about how they learn best, I formally surveyed 236 students. In the survey, I asked students to write about what effective teachers do, and you will see quotes from these surveys throughout the book. Much of my understanding of good teaching has also come from my roles as a teacher trainer and instructional coach. I have worked with teachers in Illinois and Texas, in schools spanning the gamut from high-poverty to affluence. I have worked in inner-city, suburban, and rural schools. Through my work as a coach and mentor, I have had the privilege of observing some extraordinary educators who have had a positive impact on the students they serve. As I observed and talked with these teachers, I recorded their behaviors and strategies that resulted in high levels of student engagement and success in the classroom. In analyzing this wealth of data, I found that these accomplishments in the classroom transfer to high levels of student achievement on standardized tests. Putting observation and test data together, I have reached the conclusion that the teachers whose students achieved at the highest levels share some common teaching practices, and these practices are the foundation for the rest of this book.

Here are seven "secrets of success" shared by the high-performing reading teachers:

What Effective Reading Teachers Do (The Seven Secrets of Success)

1. Provide explicit instruction on the active reading skills necessary for comprehension.
2. Guide students in small, flexibly grouped clusters in daily practice of these skills.
3. Give students opportunities to communicate about what they are reading.
4. Require students to read in class and outside of class, and hold students accountable for this reading.
5. Teach students to set goals and monitor student progress through assessment.
6. Train students to practice productive behavior during independent and collaborative learning.
7. Maintain a student-centered, positive, and safe classroom environment.

Again, my research in comparing student test scores with teacher practices showed me that these seven practices result in higher student achievement, and wider research also validates the positive effects of these practices on student achievement. Throughout the rest of this book, you will learn blended (online and face-to-face) approaches to practicing these seven secrets to success in the reading classroom. I will also share the wider research that supports the incorporation of each of these elements in your classroom.

Chapter One Summary

- ➤ In the flipped reading block, students watch a mini-lesson at home that provides explicit instruction. Then, the teacher provides students with a variety of active learning experiences during class.

- ➤ The teacher provides a blend of online and face-to-face learning experiences within the classroom.

- ➤ Studies have demonstrated that blended learning raises achievement more than purely face-to-face learning or purely online learning.

- ➤ Flexible grouping of students includes a mixture of ability-based groups, interest-based groups, student-led groups, and teacher-led groups. Combining experiences in all of these groupings with independent reading and writing experiences makes for rich and engaging learning.

- ➤ Ideas presented in this book come from my own teaching experiences, from student input, and from my observations of other teachers in my roles as a teacher trainer and instructional coach. These ideas are also supported by wider research.

- ➤ The seven secrets of success shared by teachers whose students attained high levels of achievement are the foundation for this book.

CHAPTER TWO

Explicit Instruction in the Form of Flipped Mini-Lessons

A Case for Explicit Instruction

Reading achievement often flatlines before the start of fourth grade. Yale University researchers found that three-fourths of students who struggle in third grade still struggle in high school (as cited in "Early Warning! . . . ," 2010). Why? Many of the upper elementary, middle school, and high school teachers with whom I have worked say that they really don't know how to teach comprehension. One of the problems I have observed is that reading and English teachers are typically people who enjoy reading and who naturally interact with text without thinking about it. Teachers may find it hard to explain how to employ reading strategies when they exercise these strategies on a subconscious level. However, individuals who struggle with reading must become metacognitive. They must think about their thinking and reflect on their application of active reading strategies. By doing this, they will learn to do what skilled readers do.

In order for students to learn how to read actively, the teacher must provide constant modeling of what skilled readers do. Research supports explicit teaching of comprehension skills. In a report from the U.S. Department of Education Institute of Education Sciences, positive, statistically significant correlations were made between explicit comprehension strategy instruction and test scores (James-Burdumy, Deke, Lugo-Gil, Carey, Hershey, Gersten, Newman-Gonchar, Dimino, & Haymond, 2010). Students benefit when teachers model for them the strategies for learning how to determine meaning of unknown words, make connections with text, decide what information in text is important, and make valid inferences. Teachers whom I have coached understand the need for this practice, but they express that they need to know what it looks like in the classroom.

> ## A Student's Perspective
>
> " I learn best when my teacher shows me how she learns something. "
> —*Henry, middle-school student*

How to Flip a Reading Mini-Lesson

You know from Chapter One the importance of creating small reading groups in your classroom. Therefore, you might ask: "Am I going to need to create mini-lessons that explicitly teach reading strategies for each reading group in my class?" The answer is no. Remember that you are teaching what good readers do as they read. Your explicit, whole-class teaching will provide a think-aloud that will show students, how to apply strategies to help them actively engage with text. These strategies should be applicable to any text, on any subject, at any level of difficulty. All students, for instance, must learn to make inferences about characters based on what the characters say and do. Whether reading *Where the Wild Things Are* or *Moby Dick*, readers use the same basic strategies for successfully making evidence-based inferences. Even though students will eventually practice strategies with a variety of texts in small groups, you can model the strategies by using an accessible text and letting them hear you think aloud.

> ## A Student's Perspective
>
> " Online tutorials in a flipped classroom helped me practice more and learn the material better. "
> —*Kelly, high-school student*

In a traditional classroom, you would think aloud in front of the students in the classroom. In a flipped classroom, you can record yourself with a flip cam or make a screencast using visuals and text along with your voice. Don't worry about spending a great deal of time on these lessons. They should be short, and the videos don't need to be of professional quality.

So, let's say your objective is this: Students will be able to make an evidence-based inference. To guide students in mastering this skill, you must provide explicit instruction. One way you could provide this explicit instruction is to create a screencast in which you think aloud as you examine text. Students can then watch your screencast online.

Here are the steps you could go through to make your screencast:

1. Choose a strategy that will help students learn the skill you've chosen. If you want them to make an evidence-based inference, you could, for instance, create a visual that shows the process of making an inference.

> Go online to see a demonstration of how to create a screencast for a flipped mini-lesson. See page 154 for details.

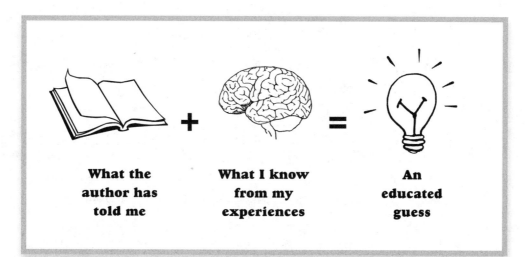

| What the author has told me | **+** | What I know from my experiences | **=** | An educated guess |

2. Write a script to go with the visual. The script might read, "When I make an inference, I first think about what the author has told me. To that, I add what I know from my experiences. When I put both of those pieces together, I can make an educated guess, or an inference."

3. Select a short text for students to read before they watch the recorded mini-lesson, for example, a poem. Before watching my example video lesson on making inferences (available online; see page 154 for details on how to access), I asked students to read Langston Hughes's poem "Mother to Son" (1994).

4. Next, write a script of a think-aloud to go with the text. Here is the script for my Langston Hughes think-aloud:

I am going to apply the steps of the inference-making strategy to the words in Langston Hughes's "Mother to Son." The narrator compares her life to a staircase, and in the second line she tells the reader that the stair has not been made of crystal. In my experience, anything with crystals, like a crystal chandelier, is luxurious and enjoyed by people with wealth. Based on this prior understanding and what the author has told me, I can make an educated guess that the mother is not wealthy. Then, in the third and fourth lines, the poet tells me that the mother's staircase has had tacks and splinters in it. I know that stepping on tacks and splinters is painful, so I can use what the author has told me combined with my own experiences to make an educated guess that the mother's life has been painful or difficult. Finally, the narrator describes the torn up boards, describing a dilapidated staircase, which would be dangerous. Adding this to my experience, I can make an evidence-based guess that the mother's life has been fraught with danger.

> Go online to view model flipped mini-lessons on
>
> ▶ Making Inferences
>
> ▶ Finding the Main Idea
>
> ▶ Using a Test-Taking Strategy
>
> ▶ Analyzing Literary Techniques
>
> See page 154 for details on how to access.

5. After you have gathered your visuals and text, and you have written your script, you are ready to record. You have many software choices for recording your screencast. (Download Technology Tools for the Flipped Reading Block: An Annotated List of Resources from the online resources; see page 154 for details on how to access.) Most screencasting tools allow you to annotate, underline, or highlight.

6. Finally, decide where students will access your video or screencast. You can post your recording on YouTube and share the link with your students, or you

can post the video directly on a learning management system (LMS). You can read about options for learning management systems in Technology Tools for the Flipped Reading Block: An Annotated List of Resources, available online; see page 154 for details on how to access.

Group Posts   Filter posts by ⌄

Mrs. Morgan to ■ 8th grade reading
Inference Video

| Turned In (7) | Due Nov 19, 2014 |

Watch the video on inferencing and come prepared to discuss it tomorrow. After that, try your hand at these riddles at the link below.

phil tulga — *music through the curriculum*
Inference Riddle Game by Phil and David Tulga
philtulga.com
📖 14

Inference video
Embed
📖 15
View Embed source

Screenshot of flipped mini-lesson posted on an Edmodo LMS.

Modeling How to Watch a Flipped Mini-Lesson

Bergmann and Sams (2012) devote time during the early part of the school year to training students on watching the videos and using the pause and rewind button to their advantage.

You, too, might start the year by watching some videos with your students. As you watch with your class, you can model by thinking aloud, pausing the video at times and saying, "I don't understand this part of the video, so I am going to rewind and watch the confusing section again." When you pause, you might even demonstrate note-taking in response to the video.

A Student's Perspective

“ Don't make us guess. We actually need specific instructions before we can focus on the learning. ”
—*Anastasia, high-school student*

Gradually, you will release students to watch the videos on their own, but you will want to be vigilant about creating formative assessments that show you whether students demonstrate an understanding of the concepts you have presented in the videos.

Accountability for Learning From the Flipped Mini-Lesson

Again, one of the benefits of the flipped classroom is that students can watch a lesson over and over until they feel they "get" it. This prevents you from feeling the need to reinforce learning for some while others patiently (or sometimes, impatiently) wait.

However, some students may struggle with a mini-lesson delivered by video. They may need to ask you in person to explain the strategy in a different way. To know which students require additional support after watching the video, you should assess their learning.

You have several options for formative assessment of students' learning.

> ## A Student's Perspective
>
> " When other students don't understand a concept that I already understand, I get frustrated because the teacher has to explain it again. I feel like I could be learning, but I have to wait. When the teacher puts the explanation online, students only have to watch it as many times as necessary. "
>
> —*Jeff, middle-school student*

1. **Transfer of Learning to New Text**—Have students transfer what they learned from your think-aloud to another text. For example, after students watched my flipped mini-lesson on the first five lines of "Mother to Son," I asked them to make another inference using the sixth line of the same poem. Utilizing a discussion board, I posted the assignment, requiring students to use the strategy from the think-aloud mini-lesson and write about the inference they made. Before the next class day, I read their responses and then created a follow-up mini-lesson for a group of students whose formative assessments demonstrated that they did not understand the strategy.

2. **Entrance Ticket**—Another way to assess is through an "entrance ticket," a short student response to a teacher question or prompt. This response provides teachers with a formative assessment that can be used

to inform the day's instruction. For example, using "Mother and Son," I would begin the post-video lesson by projecting the next line of the poem on an interactive whiteboard. Then, utilizing a chat tool, I would ask students to send a message that shows how they made an inference using the sixth line of the poem. (You can find examples of chat tools in Technology Tools for the Flipped Reading Block: An Annotated List of Resources, available online; see page 154 for details on how to access.) If not all students in the classroom have digital devices, you can create an entrance ticket that is a pencil-and-paper task.

3. **Guided Notes or Summary**—Some teachers who require students to watch videos will ask them to take guided notes in a journal or have each student post a summary of the lecture on a discussion board.

4. **Short Quiz**—Students can demonstrate their mastery by taking a short quiz. You might post the quiz on a learning management system or administer the quiz using a chat tool.

In talking with teachers who have found success with flipped classrooms, I have realized that some type of accountability measure must be in place to guarantee that students are watching the videos and learning from them.

Solutions for Students Without Personal Computers or Internet Access

Teachers must consider how students without personal computers or Internet access can watch the flipped mini-lessons. I know teachers who have created several solutions to this problem, such as:

▶ Allow students without the technology at home to watch the videos on school computers before school, during lunch, during an Advisory time, or after school.

▶ Post the videos to YouTube so students can watch them on any smartphone.

▶ Ask parents to donate old phones for students to use to watch the videos.

As a reading teacher, I typically focus on one or two skills a week. Therefore, it is not necessary to create a mini-lesson video for each school night. One or two mini-lessons a week may be all you need, and therefore the time commitment required of students is not an unreasonable one.

Chapter Two Summary

> ▶ Blended instruction can take the form of video-recorded think-alouds that students watch at home combined with in-class, collaborative follow-up lessons.

> ▶ By flipping your mini-lessons, students can watch your explicit instruction over and over until they "get" it.

> ▶ Putting an accountability piece in place ensures that students watch your flipped lessons. It also gives you a formative assessment that lets you know which students need additional support.

CHAPTER THREE

Whole-Group Guided Practice as a Follow-Up to Flipped Lessons

Moving from "I Do" to "We Do"

The purpose of the flipped classroom is not simply for students to watch a video. Instead, it is to free up time in class so that they can explore the content at a deeper level. In a blended model, online learning is combined with face-to-face learning, and the exploration of the content from the video can happen in the classroom. When teaching reading, the "I do; we do; you do" gradual release process has been shown to improve literacy and achievement (Pearson & Gallagher, 1983; Fisher & Frey, 2003; Fisher & Frey, 2007). The video is the "I do" part. You might want to reinforce your flipped mini-lesson with a brief whole-class, face-to-face lesson. Doing so lets students work with you in the "we do" part of the process before you send them off on their own to work independently in the "you do" stage. When students have already watched a mini-lesson at home, the playing field is leveled before your face-to-face mini-lesson begins. The higher-ability readers may have needed

Go online to see a video of whole-group guided practice as a follow-up to a flipped lesson. See page 154 for details.

to watch your online lesson only once, whereas your struggling readers will have had the opportunity to watch the lesson multiple times. Therefore, you will not risk disengaging your more advanced readers while you provide multiple repetitions and reteachings for students who need extra help. Your face-to-face mini-lesson might, therefore, just be a quick review before giving students in-class time for skill practice.

For this quick face-to-face follow-up lesson, you will want to make sure that students have opportunities to interact with each other and you in small spurts. Here is what a follow-up mini-lesson might look like. First, to model the process of inferring from text, you may guide the whole class as you read together a short excerpt of a story projected on the interactive whiteboard.

1. As you read along with students, highlight one character's actions, for instance, "Sam pounded his fists and demanded more pie."

2. Ask the class, "What inference can you make about Sam based on his actions?"

3. Have students interact with the content and each other by turning to a partner to respond to the question.

4. After giving students time to talk to their partners, bring the class back together for a whole-group discussion during which students share what they discussed during the partner talk. One student might say, "Sam's actions show that he is spoiled because I have seen spoiled children have temper tantrums when they don't get their way." Another student might say, "I think Sam has a bad temper because I have seen people with bad tempers pound their fists while they make demands."

From the same passage, you might highlight a character's words and guide students in making an inference about a character based on dialogue. Again, time to process with a partner or small group is a critical piece of face-to-face mini-lessons. As I pointed out earlier, the face-to-face time is the "we do" of the "I do; we do; you do" approach. Therefore, you want to let students practice with their peers during this time, while you facilitate as a guide on the side.

What you have done in this lesson is show students how to interact with text. After all, the difference between skilled readers and unskilled readers is all about how they interact with text. Skilled readers have a conversation with the text in their heads the whole time they are reading. When Sam pounds his fists, skilled readers say to themselves, "Man, this character has an out-of-control temper." Skilled readers may not even realize that they are having this internal conversation, but they are. Unskilled readers disconnect from text. They try to take in the text passively, but it just doesn't stick. As students have conversations with partners, they learn how to have conversations in their heads with text.

The example flipped lesson aligns with the example objective, which is that students will be able to make evidence-based inferences. You have gone through the "I do; we do" parts of the process by doing the following:

- ► **I do:** Providing explicit instruction through the video—reading text and thinking aloud as you model the process of making an inference

- ► **We do:** Guiding pairs of students in making inferences in the face-to-face follow-up to the video.

Following the gradual release model, you would now move to the "you do," having students work on mastering the reading skill independently in teacher-assigned, as well as student-selected, texts. Before you move onto that step, let's back up and talk about strategies for managing the partner practice in the follow-up to flipped mini-lessons. Putting this critical piece in place will save you frustration during the collaborative learning time.

Procedures to Manage Partner Practice

When I first began giving students more opportunities to talk and work in pairs, I saw increased engagement, but I also began to see some behavior problems. Because I had not yet learned to use specific language and routines to guide students during collaborative learning, the line between when it was appropriate to talk and when it was not became blurred. I would give students chances to talk with partners, but when I needed to call them back together as a whole group or to move into silent reading or writing time, they wouldn't stop talking. Even when I raised my voice, their voices continued. This became frustrating to both me and the students, and I found myself wasting time just trying to bring students back.

To create a well-managed, active, learning environment, a teacher must set up specific procedures that he or she puts into practice during the first days of school. The students need to know the behaviors that will allow them to learn in this active and authentic way.

> ### A Student's Perspective
>
> " A good teacher has to be in control.
> —*Katie, middle-school student* "

Do you remember learning about Pavlov's dogs in psychology class? After repeatedly hearing a bell right before they were fed, the dogs developed a learned response to the point that they began to salivate when they heard the bell, even before they saw the food.

Pavlov's work showed that repeated exposure to specific stimuli can elicit a specific and desired response. You can do the same thing in your classroom. You can develop specific language to let students know when it is time to talk. I like the following phrases: "You may turn to your partner and talk now" and "You may talk with your group now." I use this specific language over and over. I train the students to listen for those words before beginning their academic conversations. I also develop a signal for bringing students back to the whole-group discussion. I count out loud from the number five (or ten) backwards, or I use nonverbal cues and count with my fingers. Students know that this is the signal to wrap up a conversation. I expect absolute quiet at the number one.

You also want to develop specific routines for movement in the class. Since it benefits students to collaborate with a variety of partners, you will want to have procedures in place so that they can move to meet with those partners and groups in an orderly fashion.

A student can talk to the person sitting beside him or her, commonly known as the "shoulder partner." For this discussion, students don't need to move from their desks.

There are times, though, when students do need to move. Sitting in a desk all day simply goes against their nature. It literally causes them physical pain as sitting puts pressure on skeletal growth plates. Moving also sends oxygen to the brain, making learning easier.

For that reason, letting students move in the simplest ways as they work with partners can be very beneficial for you and your students. Teachers are often terrified of this idea because they fear losing control of the classroom. The teachers I have coached have been surprised to experience *more* control when they provide these opportunities. Later, I will demonstrate the kind of particular language that is essential to use if this activity is to work. Without that language, chaos could result.

A Student's Perspective

> " Teachers should let kids be kids who talk, socialize, and GET UP out of their seats. "
>
> —*George, middle-school student*

Standing/Sitting Pairs

One partner combination that I have always loved is one I call standing/sitting pairs. I ask students to migrate north or south. Here is how it works:

1. Half of the class, or the students on the north side of the class, have the chance to "migrate" first. Those who migrate might take on the function of teachers.

2. The "teachers" get out of their seats ("Ah, what a relief," they think to themselves), and find a "sitting" partner on the other side of the room.

3. Then, the "teacher" explains something to his or her sitting partner.

Through this activity, I accomplish several objectives at one time. First, I give students an opportunity to move their bodies. What a gift to my students! Second, I give students the chance to teach their ideas to others. Brain researcher Edgar Dale (1946) demonstrates in his Cone of Experience that we remember 90% of what we teach, while we remember only 10% of what is taught to us.

Now let's look at the language that will eliminate chaos and allow these activities to work. In the following script, I demonstrate the use of clear expectations and precise language to instruct students as they move and talk in a classroom.

"Those of you seated on the north side of the classroom are now going to migrate south and, without talking, find a partner. When I tell you to do so, you will rise from your desks and move to the other side of the room. You will then find a partner. You are to stand in front of your partner's desk until I give the verbal cue to begin teaching. Does everyone understand what to do? May I please ask for a volunteer to restate the directions?"

I call on a student, and the student repeats what all students are to do.

"If, at the end of the 15 seconds, you still do not have a partner, I will assist you by being your yenta, your matchmaker."

At this point, I see an opportune moment to make my students laugh. I tell them what a "yenta" is, and then I dramatically throw a black scarf on my head and sing an excerpt from "Matchmaker, Matchmaker" from Fiddler on the Roof.

The singing is optional, but I will say that I have observed that students seem to appreciate silly humor from teachers, so don't be afraid to take some comic risks.

"You will now have 15 silent seconds to find a partner. Please remember that these are *silent* seconds because you are to do this without talking. You will soon have an opportunity to talk as you teach your partner, but for now, please migrate silently and focus on finding a student to teach."

A Student's Perspective

" Being silly gets students' attention and helps them remember what you want them to learn. "
—Sam, middle-school student

While students move, I count with my fingers: 15, 14, 13, 12, 11, 10, 9, 8, 7, 6, 5, 4, 3, 2, 1. At one, students are standing silently in front of the desk of a partner.

"You may teach your partner now."

Of course, the next time I ask students to move, I give the south side of the room a turn to be the movers and the teachers.

Topic Partners

Another way to pair students is to assign topic partners. This is also a pairing that allows students to move. As you plan your unit, pick four or five topics. Let's say you have worked with the social studies teacher on an interdisciplinary unit, and your students are going to be reading nonfiction articles and books about early settlement in the West. You might pick the following topics: cowboys, farmers, ranchers, and Native Americans. At the beginning of the unit, ask your students to write those four topics in their notebooks, or if they use tablets or other devices, they can type the topics into a word processing or note-taking application. Then, set a time and give each student a few minutes to move around the room and find four partners—a cowboy partner, a farmer partner, a rancher partner, and a Native American partner—with whom they will communicate in spurts throughout the entire unit. As you read articles about Native Americans during this unit of study, students will converse with their Native American partners. As you study the life of the farmers in this period, students will pair up for discussions with their farmer partners, and so on.

This exercise creates some excitement about the upcoming unit, and students will be grateful to know they are going to continue to have many opportunities for movement and collaboration. You can also use topic partners to reinforce your video-recorded think-alouds. I always direct students to find their topic partners for a short debriefing activity. Sometimes, if the body language of my students lets me know that they need some movement, I might stop whatever we are doing and ask a question that students answer with their topic partners. Let's look at an example of a situation when topic partners can increase engagement.

Reading and Responding to Leveled Texts

Students have read various informational articles about how farmers in the West were driven near to madness by bed bugs. You selected short articles at differing levels so that each student in the class has an article appropriate for his or her individual reading level. Students were then assigned the task of determining the article's main idea. Each posted the main idea on the discussion board and wrote three supporting details of that main idea. Finally, each posted a modern connection to the ideas expressed in the article. While they worked online, you were able to check to see that students were mastering the skills of determining main idea and making connections in real time because you could see their responses on the discussion board. What a powerful formative assessment!

Because you have observed that students need to move after sitting and working independently at their computers on this activity, you have decided it is time to give them a chance to move.

Teaching Move: Engage Students With Topic Partners

"Since you have been reading articles about the struggles of farmers who settled in the West, you are now going to share the main idea and supporting details of your articles with your farmer partners. You will have fifteen silent seconds to meet and stand back-to-back with your farmer partner. When I see that partners are back-to-back, I will know that you are ready for academic conversations. After I give you directions to talk, you will remain standing while you share the main idea and key points of your article. Again, you will have an opportunity to talk to your partner once I have given you the signal to do so. While you are moving, though, please stay quiet. Find your partners now."

Begin counting: 15, 14, 13, 12, 11, 10, 9, 8, 7, 6, 5, 4, 3, 2, 1. Students should be standing back-to-back with farmer partners at "one."

"Thank you for remaining silent during the movement. You have all found your farmer partners. Would someone please tell us what you and your farmer partner are expected to discuss."

A student tells the class that farmer partners will discuss the main idea and supporting details of the article.

"Great. Does everyone understand what to do? Give me a thumbs up if the answer is yes and a thumbs down if the answer is no." *Look around.* "Okay. You may turn to your partner and talk now."

Engaged learners share their ideas, increase their literacy, and enjoy your class.

· ·

Reinforcing Flipped Mini-Lessons With Fun Follow-Up Lessons That Invigorate Learners

You will probably want to record some mini-lessons on word decoding strategies since these strategies support readers at all levels. Our modern learners are exposed to language everyday through Internet searches, text messaging, and even social network sites. They need skills to decode language so that they can develop in the area of literacy. It makes sense that we, as their teachers, should teach word decoding strategies.

One of the most basic word decoding strategies is understanding how prefixes can affect word meaning. The mere thought of this lesson is probably making you sigh with boredom. I remember what this lesson was like when I was a student. It would involve a list of words beginning with a particular prefix. We would write each of these words a hundred times—well, maybe it was only 20, but it felt like one hundred. Then, we would take a spelling test and a matching vocabulary test on the 20 new words at the end of the week. Misery multiplied by 20!

Literacy instruction has changed. Praise modern educational practices!!! We still understand that students need to learn about prefixes, but we know we should teach the topic in a more authentic way. As you are about to see, you can take what would typically be considered the most boring topic a teacher could possibly teach and make it highly engaging—and even fun—for students. In the following example lesson, students draw on their prior knowledge to understand the meaning of prefixes, and then have opportunities to look for interesting words with these prefixes in various texts that they are reading.

As you read this script for a follow-up lesson to my think-aloud video on prefixes, pay attention to the language. I am hoping you will be pleasantly surprised by how engaging this lesson can be just by sprinkling some collaborative learning into it.

A Student's Perspective

❝ Be strict but nice when we do activities. ❞
—*John, middle-school student*

Earlier, I mentioned the importance of using precise language when incorporating collaborative learning strategies into your classroom. I cannot emphasize how important this is! As a mentor, I have coached many teachers on using this language. I realize that, at first, it feels awkward to repeat the same language over and over until you feel like a broken record. However, it is absolutely essential that the line between when it is appropriate to talk and when it is not is crystal clear. The moment that line becomes blurred is the moment you become exasperated, which can have a really unpleasant domino effect. Students start talking when you need to give instructions or when they need to do independent reading. Your patience wanes, and as a consequence, you stop giving students opportunities to learn collaboratively. Engagement decreases. Student academic growth slows. Test scores go down. I am sure you can imagine, in this age of high accountability, what the next few falling dominoes will look like.

So, as you read this example lesson, try to visualize how engaged students are as they have fun with a topic traditionally considered boring. Really tune into the language, used repeatedly to ensure students understand when they may talk, when they may move, and when they must give their attention to the teacher. Then, picture yourself teaching lessons and watching engaged learners who grow rapidly in a safe and happy community of learners.

Using Prefixes to Decode Words

"Today, we are going to explore ways to decode words. You are going to have many chances during this lesson to talk to classmates and collaborate with them. However, there will be times when I will need you to listen to my instructions, so please only talk after I have given you explicit instructions to do so. I will say the words, 'You may turn to your partner and talk now' when it is time for you to talk and collaborate."

Teaching Move: Engage Students With Shoulder Partners

"With your shoulder partner, you will review your learning from yesterday's video about ways to decode words. I will tell you when to begin. When it is time to wind down your conversations, I will count backwards from five. Make sure it is quiet when I reach the number one. Would someone please tell the class what the partners will do when I give you the cue to start talking? (*Student answers.*) Good! Is everyone ready? You may turn to your partner and talk now."

Students share decoding strategies with partners.

To wind down partner talk, say:

"5, 4, 3, Wind down conversations, 2, 1. Thank you for demonstrating silence at one. Please raise your hand if you can think of ways in which we can decode words."

Call on individual students. Students provide several different ways to decode words.

Teaching Move: Challenge Students to Generate Examples and Infer Meanings of Prefixes

"Julia answered that one way to decode words is to look for prefixes. Look at the prefix written on the board. I am going to ask you and your shoulder partner to think of as many words as you can that begin with the prefix *un-*. I have invited you to an online chat. One partner should type the words as you think of them, and I will project the words on the screen for all to see. After you have thought of three or four words, please look at the list generated by your classmates and see if you can determine the meaning of the prefix. Who can tell the class the work you and your partner will do once I tell you it is time to collaborate?"

Student answers, "We will think of as many words as we can that begin with the prefix un-. *Then, we will try to figure out the meaning of the prefix."*

The Flipped Reading Block © 2015 by Gina Pasisis, Scholastic Teaching Resources

"Great. Does everyone understand? Okay. You may turn to your partner and talk now."

After students have generated a list of words, begin counting from 5 to 1.

Wind down the partner talk by saying:

"5, 4. During this countdown, you should wind down conversations. At one, you should be silent. 3, 2, 1. Thank you for demonstrating silence at one. Look at the words generated by the class. What did you and your partner decide that the prefix *un-* means?"

(Call on students with raised hands.)

Teaching Move: Engage Students With Standing Partners to Apply Knowledge

"You figured it out. The prefix *un-* means *not*."

"Now, you are going to have an opportunity to create a 'what not to do list' using words that begin with *un-*. For example, you may demonstrate what *not* to do if you want to be a good player on the soccer team. Do not:

1. *Un*tie your shoelaces.
2. Jump up and down *un*necessarily.
3. Run around the field like an *un*ruly child.

"For this activity you are going to move and work with a standing partner. Without talking, you will take your device and walk around the room in search of a partner. When you find your partner, you will stand back to back with that partner until I give instructions to talk. When I say to, you may find your partner. Again, please do not talk during this transition. You will have a chance to talk soon, though. All students may now get out of your seats and find a standing partner. You have 15 seconds to do so. Go. 15, 14, 13, 12, 11, 10, 9, 8, 7, 6, 5, 4, 3, 2, 1. Is anyone without a partner?"

At this point, you play matchmaker if necessary.

Continue by saying:

"Okay. Now that everyone has a partner, will someone please repeat the directions."

A student says, "We make a 'what not to do' list using words that begin with the prefix un-."

"Great! You and your partner can find a place to sit and work in the classroom. Feel free to make your list funny. After you and your partner create your list, please post it to the online chat. You may turn to your partner and talk now."

As you walk around, lean in and listen to conversations so that students will know you are holding them accountable for staying on task. Notice students having fun as they work creatively and find amusement in each other's responses on the projected screen.

To wind down this activity, say:

"5, 4, 3, 2, 1."

(At this point, students should know that this is the cue to wind down conversations.)

Teaching Move: Check Understanding

"After working with words that begin with *un-*, do you feel as though you understand now how you can use this prefix to assist you in decoding words? Give me a thumbs up close to the chest if the answer is yes. Give me a thumbs down if the answer is no."

(Scan the room.)

Finally, to close the lesson, say:

"That you are quick learners is UNDENIABLE, which means, of course, that it is not deniable! Please move back to your original locations in ten seconds. 10, 9, 8, 7, 6, 5, 4, 3, 2, 1."

• •

When I have taught this lesson, students always laugh, and I love that. I laugh with them, and I love that, too. I imagine that they think to themselves, "This is a fun class. I am learning so much."

You have now taken a very simple, yet important, follow-up to a recorded, flipped mini-lesson, and you have made it fun and highly engaging by letting students collaborate and be creative. Planning engaging lessons like this does not have to be time consuming, but you must establish routines if your class is to be successful with talking and movement. As I wrote earlier, you may feel like a broken record, but using specific language as a cue for when it is an appropriate time to talk will allow you to conduct activities like this one all year long without losing control or pulling your hair out. Again, make perfectly clear the line between when students should

A Student's Perspective

" I like a teacher who is light-hearted but who still keeps us focused on the lesson.
—*Tommy, high-school student* "

talk and when students should listen. Without specific language that you use over and over and over, that line can easily become fuzzy, and collaborative learning will be frustrating for you and your students. We don't want that!

You can find many ways for students to collaborate in everyday, ordinary lessons. The point of the previous example is to show that you can make any lesson, even a traditionally boring one, exciting by spicing it up with a little collaborative learning. Having procedures in place for managing talking and movement will make this possible.

What Skills Should Be Explicitly Taught?

Through your flipped mini-lessons, you will model ways that skilled readers interact with text. By observing your think-alouds, students will see what good readers do. So, you might be asking, "What should I model in my think-alouds? Just what do skilled readers do?"

What Skilled Readers Do

▶ Set a purpose for their reading.

▶ Make use of text features and visuals to aid them in understanding the main text.

▶ Self-assess continually as they read. They check for understanding, reread, and use context clues to determine word meaning and make sense of complex text. They use word decoding strategies to determine the meanings of unknown words.

▶ Create a movie in their heads as they read. They make use of the author's language to visualize text.

▶ Look for text patterns that aid in comprehension.

▶ Search for big ideas so they understand the author's message (main idea, purpose, and theme).

▶ Make connections between the text and their own lives, the text and the world, and the text and other texts. This constant synthesis of information while reading makes the reader actively engaged.

▶ Allow text to spark their natural intellectual curiosity, which leads to questions.

▶ Distinguish between essential and non-essential ideas in text.

- Separate fact from opinion. They are discerning consumers of textual information.

- Make inferences, draw conclusions, and make predictions based on text evidence.

- Analyze an author's literary elements and techniques as a way to enhance understanding and appreciation of text.

(Diamond, Honig, & Gutlohn, 2013; Duke & Pearson, 2002; Duke, Pearson, Strachan, & Billman, 2011; Wilhelm, 2001)

By modeling what skilled readers do through think-alouds and explicit instruction, and by giving students continual opportunities to practice, you give every reader a chance at success. In the next two chapters, you will see how online tools and face-to-face collaboration in small groups will help students observe both you and other students use active reading strategies. You will also see how these tools can encourage student reflection as they practice the strategies independently.

Chapter Three Summary

- The "we do" of the "I do; we do; you do" model can take place as a face-to-face, follow-up lesson that includes collaborative activities.

- You can maintain a positive environment during collaborative learning by putting specific structures in place.

- Modeling what skilled readers do will help your students master critical reading skills.

Guiding and Facilitating Reading Instruction in Small Groups

Flexible Reading Groups

Teachers cannot simply provide explicit instruction and just hope that it sinks into the brains of their students. After students see their teacher model the instruction, they need to practice with the teacher as a guide, facilitator, and continual assessor of their understanding. In Chapter Three, you read about whole-group guided practice, which is an effective way for a teacher to expose students to a general reading strategy. The next teacher step during the "we do" stage involves drilling deeper to individualize instruction based on specific needs. This can happen when the teacher works with small groups. Studies have shown that small-group, guided skills practice has a positive, statistically significant impact on student achievement (James-Burdumy et al, 2010; Paratore & Indrisano, 2003).

A Student's Perspective

> I know my teacher has a whole room full of kids to teach, but I appreciate the times when he gives me personal attention.
> —*Nicholas, middle-school student*

While homogeneous-ability grouping may give teachers the opportunity to provide students with instruction at their individualized zones of reading readiness, some studies have shown that "students placed in low-achieving small groups often experience low self-esteem and negative attitudes toward reading and learning" (Paratore & Indrisano, 2003, p. 566). What to do? Provide experiences in which students work in a variety of flexible grouping arrangements for a variety of purposes.

I have the utmost admiration for Irene Fountas and Gay Su Pinnell, who have influenced the practices of many teachers through their collaborative efforts in the creation of Guided Reading, a program that encourages teachers to guide small clusters of students reading at similar levels of readiness. The program focuses on helping students develop fluency and comprehension through teacher-led, small-group instruction. This personalized approach allows students to read individualized text that is just right for each student's level of readiness. Fountas and Pinnell consider the "just right" level to be text that is accessible, yet challenging (1996).

I also greatly respect Harvey Daniels (2002), whose ideas gave birth to Literature Circles, a model that encourages student-directed learning. In the Literature Circles approach, students choose texts based on interest rather than reading level. They meet with others reading the same text and engage in authentic conversations about literature.

> ## A Student's Perspective
>
> " When I read a book that is too easy, it is boring. I can't even find one word I don't know. "
> —*Claire, intermediate student*

As I stated earlier, some research demonstrates that teachers should work with students in homogeneous clusters. For instance, the research conducted by Karen Rogers (1991) shows that ability grouping and instruction specific to the readiness levels of students have a dramatic impact on student achievement. In fact, in her study, children in homogenous-ability groups outperformed children who were not grouped by three or more months in just one school year. This research supports a model through which the teacher forms groups based on student achievement and student ability data.

Other research shows that students should have opportunities for rich, meaningful, authentic discussions about books that students choose based on interest rather than reading level. Opportunities to select literature based on personal interest and to discuss it in small groups motivate students to read and raise achievement levels on tests (Davis, Resta, Davis, & Comacho, 2001). Using this research, a teacher might choose to form Literature Circles.

I suggest that you blend the very best parts of these two approaches to reading instruction and use an online component as support. What does this mean?

The Flipped Reading Block © 2015 by Gina Pasisis, Scholastic Teaching Resources

- Students will be a part of two groups at a time.
- These groups will be fluid rather than fixed.

This may seem as if it would become confusing, but I have watched many teachers manage flexible grouping beautifully. With some advance planning, the transitions can be very smooth. A strategic teacher moves students from one group and activity to the next, and he or she trains them to do so in a way that is orderly.

Students enjoy the chance to work as a part of several groups. They appreciate being a part of a group that offers the appropriate degree of challenge, but they also like to be part of a group that shares a similar reading interest. With flexible grouping, we differentiate instruction without the risk of damaging students. Some of us might remember the early days of reading groups, where some groups were "bluebirds" and others "buzzards." The bluebirds never mingled with the buzzards. In this situation, it always seemed that the bluebirds flew higher and higher while the buzzards swooped lower and lower. With flexible grouping, all students have the chance to fly higher toward their reading goals.

In the structure that I am suggesting, each student is part of a *strategy practice group* based on reading level. In this group, students meet with the teacher in face-to-face sessions during which the teacher guides students through strategy practice. Students are also part of this ability-based small group on a discussion board, where they participate in online discussions. Teachers can provide online guidance to this group of students through this forum.

> ## A Student's Perspective
>
> " I enjoy doing different class activities with different students. "
> —*José, middle-school student*

In addition to being a member of a strategy practice group, each student is also part of a book club based on student choice. The teacher provides a list of high-interest novels and nonfiction books, and each student joins with others who have chosen to read and discuss the same book. For these groups, the teacher acts more as facilitator so that students have the opportunity for student-directed discussions about literature to which they are emotionally connected. Again, the teacher gives the group opportunities for online and face-to-face discussions. I will provide detailed guidance for creating online discussion-board opportunities in the next chapter.

Some teachers with whom I have worked have expressed concern about students becoming confused as they read multiple texts, but I have never observed this to be a problem. Think of how we, as adults, read authentically. We rarely focus on one text at a time. I know that I am always juggling professional books and journals, novels, newspapers, leisure magazines, and a plethora of online articles as I research topics of interest.

Students will read three to four texts at a time.

1. **Whole-class texts**—As you model strategies for mastering skills and present those during mini-lessons, you will choose short texts that the entire class will read.

2. **Strategy practice group texts**—You will also choose these texts for your groups. Since these clusters will be grouped homogeneously by reading-readiness levels, you might have three to five groups. Sometimes, strategy practice groups will read different texts aligned to reading levels. Other times, the entire class may read the same text, but you will provide varying levels of support to groups based on need. You might choose shorter texts for these groups. For instance, you could pull excerpts from books, short stories, or articles that fit well with specific strategies students need to practice. In the "old school" style of teaching reading, teachers felt a need to familiarize students with particular stories and novels, but learning about a novel is not what matters here. Instead, students must learn strategies that help them master skills that good readers possess.

3. **Book club texts**—In addition to whole-class readings as a part of mini-lessons and texts designed to help students build skills in their strategy practice groups, students will read both fiction and nonfiction books as part of their book clubs. I recommend that you invest time and research in carefully selecting book sets for these book discussion groups. If you select well-written literature proven to engage readers of particular age groups, you cannot fail at ensuring that students will read. Students *will* read if text is irresistible.

4. **Independent reading text**—At times, students may even read a fourth text: a student-selected, independent reading book.

In summary, as students read different texts for a variety of purposes, they will collaborate with different groups. Here is a table showing the differences between the strategy practice groups and book clubs:

STRATEGY PRACTICE GROUPS	BOOK CLUBS
Homogeneous groups based on reading level	Heterogeneous groups based on student choice
Groups focus on strategy practice and mastery of skills	Groups engage in authentic, student-led discussions

STRATEGY PRACTICE GROUPS	BOOK CLUBS
Teacher guides the small groups online (through a group discussion board) and face-to-face (during in-class meetings)	Teacher acts as facilitator as groups discuss their books online (through a group discussion board) and face-to-face (during in class meetings)
Students read fiction and nonfiction book excerpts, short stories, and articles	Students read books (in both fiction and nonfiction genres)

Forming Strategy Practice Groups

For your strategy practice groups, you will create clusters according to reading levels. You might cluster students in groups of four to six learners. Many states require standardized tests that provide data about student reading level, indicating whether a student reads below, at, or above level. Your district may use other standardized assessments that yield that information. One such example is the Northwest Evaluation Association's Measures of Academic Progress. This assessment gives national percentiles for each student along with a key to student Lexile levels, which will help you as you choose texts for students to read. BookWizard is one resource that can help you find Lexiles or the grade level of equivalent of books. For other resources, see Technology Tools for the Flipped Reading Block: An Annotated List of Resources, available online; see page 154 for details on how to access.

Informational Text for Strategy Practice Groups

Think about what adults read: newspapers, journals, informational e-mails, and a variety of explanatory texts on topics ranging from how to program a television to how to take a medication. Yes, we enjoy our fiction, but our everyday reading is primarily informational. Despite what we read in the real world, we have, as reading teachers, traditionally spent the majority of our reading classroom time focused on fictional text. Learners love fictional text, and I am in no way suggesting that we throw it out. If we can find text that students will read because they love it, we have won half of the battle because students only practice reading skills when they actually read. However, we owe it to our learners to give them opportunities to read informational text, the type of text they will need to tackle when they enter their adult lives in the real world. A mixture of engaging fiction and nonfiction will provide a well-rounded experience for your learners.

Where do we find short informational texts at a variety of levels so that we can differentiate for diverse learners within a classroom? The online world is filled with exciting options. You will find a list of options in Technology Tools for the Flipped Reading Block: An Annotated List of Resources, available online; see page 154 for details on how to access.

Some resources online are free, but others require a subscription. Talk with your media specialist about what resources your school already has available for teachers and students to access and do some research to find what you may be able to order and use. Current, relevant articles will make the experience of reading informational text more meaningful for your students.

Working With Strategy Practice Groups: What Does It Look Like?

During this section, I will focus on what your face-to-face time with students in small strategy groups will look like. I will discuss more details about the online piece and the student-led book club discussion piece in the next chapter.

Each day, you will pull aside several small groups of students to work on specific strategies. What, you might ask, will the other students in the class be doing while you are working with the small groups? They will:

- practice independent, active reading strategies

- whisper-read with a partner

- participate in Reader's Theater

- listen and follow along with an audio recording

- reflect and write about their reading experiences online

- communicate with other students online

> Go online to see videos of strategy practice groups in action. See page 154 for details.

In the next few chapters, I will give you the details on how to structure these activities.

For now, though, I will concentrate on what will happen when you conduct a small-group session. I really understood the power of small groups once I started working with them.

Interacting with a group of four to six students provides a much stronger teacher/student connection than working with a class of 20 to 30 students. From both my experience as a teacher and my observation of other teachers, I have witnessed students responding in positive ways to teachers who work with them in a small-group setting. While students might find themselves tempted to disconnect in a large class due to the feeling of anonymity, they seem to stay more focused in a small group. They make eye contact with the teacher and listen actively to what he or she has to say. They all participate and respond to one another. Student engagement soars! I have also observed that students work harder in preparation for meeting with the teacher in the small-group setting. What was for many years called the "invisible student" fails to exist in a small group.

Before students meet with the teacher in a small group, the teacher may assign a book excerpt, a short story excerpt, or a nonfiction article for students to read. The chosen text should align to the focus of the small-group meeting. To determine the focus of the small-group time, the teacher will consider specific needs of that group of students. For example, a formative assessment may show that a certain group needs guided practice in determining patterns in text, so that could be the teacher's focus with this group during the small-group meeting. While they meet, the teacher can guide students as they practice strategies to build literacy skills. The teacher might ask questions about the text or listen to students as they read parts of the text aloud. Through this guided practice, the teacher can diagnose breakdowns in comprehension, fluency, or analysis of text.

Here are some questions to consider when planning the focus of your small-group meetings:

▶ How can I use this time to reinforce the whole-group lesson?

▶ Does this group's formative assessment data demonstrate learning gaps, and how can I use this time for reteaching to close those gaps?

▶ Which reading strategies does this group need to practice? How can I use this time to facilitate that practice?

▶ Could this be a time for students to read along with me to practice fluency?

▶ How can this time be an opportunity for me to provide extension for high-ability students who need to explore content at greater levels of depth and complexity?

In addition to planning the focus of your time with groups, you might also consider logistics. It is a good idea, if possible, to have a kidney-shaped table for meetings with small groups. With you at the center in the curved part of the table, you are close to each student in the group. You can easily reach each student's text so that you can point to words or phrases in the text as students read, and you can easily maintain eye contact with each student.

Let's put all of these ideas together and look at some example lessons for small groups. For a moment, revisit the script in Chapter Three from the whole-class, face-to-face mini-lesson on prefixes (see pages 36–38). After that lesson, you may have chosen to assign various articles to strategy groups based on reading level.

You may pull one of the groups and guide them through an exercise in which they practice in response to the whole-group lesson. Here is a possible scenario.

TEACHING SCENARIO

Small-Group Follow-Up to Whole-Class Lessons

Teacher: *(to the whole group)* We are now going to explore another prefix, and, rather than telling you the meaning of it, I would like for you to discover it through reading and context clues. The prefix is *ir-*. I have projected a link to a short article. Please pull this up on your device. As you skim and scan the article, highlight words that begin with *ir-*.

As students do this, the teacher makes a sweep through the room to check on the other students who are either reading or writing about what they are reading. Then, return to the small group.

Teacher: *(to the small group)* What words did you find?

Natalie: *Irrational.*

James: *Irregular.*

Teacher: Let's start with *irrational*. Point to the word in your article.

The teacher helps students who need assistance.

Teacher: Maria, will you please read the sentence.

Maria: *His decision to fly from Waco to Austin was irrational since driving would have taken him half of the time, considering airport parking and wait time.*

Teacher: What context clues can help you determine the meaning of the word *irrational*?

Liz: Doubling the time by flying is not logical.

Teacher: Let's see what happens if you substitute *not logical* for *irrational* in that sentence.

James: It makes sense.

Teacher: Liz, you are correct. *Irrational* means *not logical*. What do you think *ir-* means now that you have determined the meaning of irrational through context clues?

Natalie: I think *ir-* means *not* and *rational* means *logical*.

Teacher: Your collaborative effort in determining the meaning of a word and prefix was impressive. Before we meet again the day after tomorrow, please read the rest of the article and determine the meaning of another word that begins with *ir-*. You may break the word down and determine the meaning through prefixes and roots, or you may use context clues. Does everyone understand the assignment?

Students respond positively.

Teacher: Thank you for your time. Head back to your seats to work on this or to read for your book clubs. You are ready for some "you do" time.

• •

Let's say you have pulled a group of students who are working on finding patterns in text. You have chosen Thurber's autobiographical piece, "The Night the Bed Fell on Father," for the group to read in preparation for this meeting.

Here is a sample script from this teacher-guided strategy practice group meeting.

TEACHING SCENARIO

Small-Group Analysis of Text Patterns

Teacher: Good morning. Did you enjoy the story?

John: I thought it was funny, especially when Briggs poured the camphor on himself.

Angelica: I got confused because so many things were happening at one time.

Teacher: I am glad you mentioned that, Angelica. We are working on mastering the skill of finding patterns in text. If you search for a pattern, you might find the text easier to comprehend. Let's consider some of the patterns we discussed earlier this week when we met. Please open the document I sent you. Luis, will you please type these patterns on the shared document as your group members remember them?

Luis: Okay.

Teacher: Thanks, Luis. What are the patterns?

Kate: Cause/effect.

Luis types this while the others in the group look at the growing list on the document.

> **Teacher:** Yes. What else?
>
> **Thomas:** Chronological order.
>
> **John:** Least to most important idea.

Luis adds these patterns.

> **Teacher:** I am glad you have remembered some of the common methods of organization. Let's read part of the story. When I say "begin," I would like for you all to whisper-read the second paragraph on page 3 as I read it. Begin.

Students read along with the teacher.

> **Teacher:** Let's pause here and reflect. After reading this passage, what pattern do you think Thurber is using and why do you think he is using it? Type or use your stylus to write a quick response on your device, and then show your response.

The teacher should make a quick sweep of the room at this point to make sure other students are on-task, then return to the small group.

Thomas shows the teacher his response. He has written: "Chronological order. Thurber used this order to show how one misunderstanding led to another one, which led to another one, and so on. A sequence that occurred in the order of the time it happened was the only logical way for Thurber to tell this story."

> **Teacher:** (*in a whisper*) You may go now to your reading spot and work on applying this strategy of looking for a pattern to the newspaper article. You are ready for "you do." You will find the link on your strategy practice group page on the discussion board.

One by one, each student shows the teacher his or her response. Since the students in this scenario have all found a pattern and logically supported it with textual evidence, they are all dismissed to work on independent reading. If one of the students had struggled on the response (the electronic exit slip), the teacher could have spent a bit more time working with that student individually.

• •

Again, as you work with small groups, the rest of the class will read independently, whisper-read with partners, listen to and follow along with audio recordings, read with other students in a reader's theater, reflect and write about their reading experiences online, or communicate with other students online. Therefore, it is essential to train students in the small group to be low talkers. This, like everything else in this structure, takes training, especially in the beginning.

I work with a strategy practice group on finding the main idea of an excerpt from a book.

When you begin working with your strategy practice groups, you should model the level at which you want the students' voices during the small-group meeting. I would suggest the barely-above-a-whisper level.

I find it helpful to keep four cards at the table. On the cards, write the following:

- ▶ "Speak up a little."
- ▶ "Just right."
- ▶ "A bit too loud."
- ▶ "Way too loud."

As students are discussing and reading, you can flash the card or move the card close to the text.

As you saw in the sample lesson, students move from working with you in a small group to transferring the skill as they are sent off to work independently. They will be able to show you their progress as they write about what they are reading on the discussion board.

Forming Book Clubs

Using online tools, you can make the formation of book clubs easy. To begin, you create a book list from which students can choose. Again, if you choose well-written literature that has been proven to engage learners of particular ages, you will have the best chance of ensuring that students actually read. Remember that getting "eyes on text" is the first step toward increasing achievement in reading. You might choose books from a particular genre for each three-to-six week period. That way, even though students are reading different books, they will all have exposure to a variety of genres throughout the school year. You might ask students if any of them have already read the books you have chosen. If they have, you could enlist their help in putting together online book reviews. Jamie Diamond, in *Literacy Lessons for a Digital World*, describes how she wants her students to "share their reading experiences with peers to foster an environment where reading becomes something we all like to talk about as if we were discussing a favorite video game or television show" (p. 123). Mrs. Diamond's students create podcasts as tools for book reviews.

The following teacher-created book review is an example of what a book review posted on your website or discussion board might look like:

The Harmonica

Author: Tony Johnston

Illustrator: Ron Mazellan

Beautifully written and illustrated, *The Harmonica* tells the poignant story of a Polish boy who is separated from his parents during the Holocaust. The boy tells how his love of music gives him joy during his happy childhood before he and his family were captured by the Nazis, and he tells how his gift of music helps him survive a concentration camp because of his commandant's appreciation of music. Most of all, his musical gift allows him to share something of hope and beauty with other prisoners.

THEME

Even in the darkest of times, the human spirit is strong and powerful.

READING AND INTEREST LEVEL

This book is suitable for fifth through eighth graders. The language is rich and poetic, and the main character is pictured to be around the middle school age.

A STUDENT'S CONNECTION

"I read this book after having studied the Holocaust in social studies. I understood this horrible period in history by seeing what someone my age experienced. I shared the story with a few of my friends, and even a 'tough' boy in my class was glassy-eyed by the end of the story."

The Flipped Reading Block © 2015 by Gina Pasisis, Scholastic Teaching Resources

If you do not have students who have read books on your list and if you do not have time to write reviews yourself, you can always post a link to a book review that you find online.

In addition to online book reviews, you might even want to set up a gallery walk to allow students to explore each of the book choices. You could hang a poster containing information about each book. Beside the poster, place a box containing copies of the book and some book reviews. In groups, the students rotate to each poster, read the information on the poster, skim through books and reviews, and discuss their predictions about the books as they are making their decisions.

I would recommend giving students a few days to consider their options. Then, they can send their choices to you through an online chat or on the discussion board.

Using that information, you can form groups of four to six students. Once you have formed your book clubs, you can announce them and create online discussion groups for the discussion board. Remember: It is okay to have more than one group reading the same book, especially if one of the books is particularly enticing to students.

Establishing a Book Club Plan

There are times when a teacher should direct and guide and times when he or she should step to the side. Unlike teacher-designed strategy practice group meetings and strategy practice group online communication, book club meetings and online discussions should be student-directed.

I learned how effective small, student-directed discussion groups could be purely by accident, just like I have learned many valuable lessons as a teacher. In the late 1980s, I attended Junior Great Books training, and I began using the shared-inquiry strategies in my classroom immediately. I recruited parents to lead book clubs in my classroom. Yes, I had made progress. I was finally giving students the chance to talk about books, but an adult still had the lead in the classroom at all times. One day, a parent volunteer was ill, so I decided to let a student lead that group. I was amazed! The students had a discussion richer than any I had heard when the parents were leading the groups. The next year, I did not recruit parents. Students led their own discussions, and I have continued this practice ever since.

For book clubs, you may provide parameters, but the students should design what the group time looks like. Before students even start reading a book, you will want them to plan a structure for their reading, reflection, and discussion. Both Harvey Daniels (2002) and Cindy O'Donnell-Allen (2006) recommend that students decide on ground rules and create goals for reading. I agree with them, and I think you can use the discussion board as the place for this to happen so that class time can be densely packed with thinking activities.

First, decide how long you would like to give the groups to complete their books. After students know the time frame, you can let them decide as a group how they would like to structure this time. You might appoint a student to be the deadlines and norms leader. Then, you can let that leader begin an online discussion with questions for the group. The leader may begin the discussion with these questions:

▶ How many pages should we read each day?

▶ What is the minimum number of times we should each post on the discussion board?

▶ What norms do you think we should set for our online and face-to-face discussions?

Anissa M. to ■ The Lightning Thief (8th grade reading)

Questions:
How many pages should we read each day?
What is the minimum number of times we should post on the discussion board?
What norms do you think we should set for our online and face-to-face discussion?

☺ ⌄ · ◯ 2 Replies · ⎘ Share   Nov 3, 2014

Samantha A. said Nov 4, 2014
1. at least 20-25 pages every day (we can decide if we need to read more a specific night).
2. 3 times a week
3.
- We have to be respectful to each other and other's opinions
- School Appropriate
- Use good grammar
- Always be kind
- Always put forward your best effort

Anissa M. said Nov 4, 2014
I agree with this Samantha and I think that we should move forward with the book today.

Online discussion to determine deadlines and norms.

Ethan T. to ◼ Slated (8th grade reading) ⚙
http://goo.gl/forms/7yOO7u28Qo

The Google form/vote that Nicolas pleaded for.

One response only for each person please!

Much
Appreciation...
Show Full Post

☺ ⌄ · Q 1 Reply · ↗ Share   Nov 4, 2014

Sarah M. said Nov 4, 2014
Thank you.

A deadline and norms leader uses a Google form to collect data.

After all students have submitted their posts, the deadlines and norms leader can decide what to do with the data. For instance, if all students except one suggest reading one chapter a day, the discussion leader can send everyone a message saying, "Most people in the group want to read one chapter a day, so we are going to go with the majority." If the students have a wide range of numbers for discussion posts per day, the discussion leader may want to average the number. For norms, let's say one student recommends that the group use a discussion ball to pass around during face-to-face discussions to prevent students from talking over one another, and another student recommends dividing discussion tickets equally among group members to give every person equal air time. The discussion leader might let all students vote on which of the two norms they wish to practice. It may take a few days of communication before the leader can put together a plan, but you should ask the leader to share that plan with you so that you can use it for accountability. You can either approve the plan or send it back with suggestions for revision (if, for instance, the deadlines are unrealistic and the norms do not sound reasonable).

Go online to see videos of book clubs in action. See page 154 for details.

For strategy practice groups, the teacher steers the conversation in the direction of the skills students need to learn. However, for face-to-face book club discussions, which are the discussions that can lead students toward the joy of reading, the teacher absolutely must step aside, no matter how desperate he or she is to intercede. By stepping aside, I don't mean moving to the teacher's desk. As a teacher, I know that temptation all too well, but the teacher's presence still maintains power even when the teacher does not dominate the conversation.

It is true that students want independence to lead their own discussions, but they still want the security that comes when teachers remain close enough to keep them safe. Teachers in this situation must walk a tight rope. On one side of the rope lies constant intervention in discussions. On the other side lies complete disconnection. To maintain the perfect balance on a tightrope that leads to student success, the teacher must stay somewhat disconnected, interjecting in conversations only when necessary.

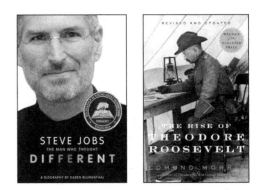

Here is an example of student discussions and the teacher's interaction with students during those discussions. For this example, book clubs have been reading biographies. One group discusses *Steve Jobs: The Man Who Thought Different* (Blumenthal, 2012) and another group discusses *The Rise of Theodore Roosevelt* (Morris, 2001).

TEACHING SCENARIO

Student-Led Book Discussion

Emma: I was amazed by the way Jobs could distort reality.

Kevin: Yeah, the way he acted like he didn't have to obey laws that other people had to obey. Like how he disregarded handicapped parking signs and parked in them.

James: I can make a connection. Really intelligent people sometimes disregard man-made laws, but they don't intend to hurt people. They are just on a different thinking level, insanely

An eighth grader leads the book club discussion.

focused on a task, and they don't always consider how their actions affect others. They don't mean to hurt people.

Jenny: You are the one who is insane, James. How could you defend a . . .

Teacher: (*in a neutral tone*) Jenny, I understand you want to make a point, but please respect the ideas of the others in your book club.

Jenny: Okay. James, I would like to respectfully disagree. (*Jenny meets eyes with the somewhat distant teacher, who offers encouragement through a gentle smile and nod.*)

Jenny: A person's intelligence does not give him the right to stomp on others, especially those who are handicapped. That is why I do not agree that what Jobs did in this situation was forgivable due to his intelligence.

The teacher, from a distance, gives an affirming nod toward Jenny and James, and then walks away toward another group.

● ●

TEACHING SCENARIO

Student-Led Book Discussion

Nick: I think Teddy Roosevelt's actions were brave. I like how Jayden wrote online that Roosevelt deserves all the manly Campbell's soup in the world.

Everyone in the group laughs.

Kate: I agree. He risked his own life when he ordered his men to charge. He did not stay behind, but he joined them.

Prakar: I must disagree with both Nick and Kate. Roosevelt's actions were completely impulsive. He really did not know what he was facing, and he put all of his men at risk when he ordered them to charge.

> ## A Student's Perspective
>
> " Give students more freedom and just guide them. "
> —*Laura, middle-school student*

The teacher, standing at a slight distance, follows the conversation by subtle turns of the neck and movement of the eyes. The discussion is animated and respectful, so the teacher has no need to interfere. After a few more comments, she moves and stands at a slight distance from another group.

● ●

As you can see from the example, the teacher's job for book clubs is to remain as distant as possible, only interjecting when the discussion moves dangerously close to going awry. In my experience, walking around the room with a gentle smile of affirmation when students look my way keeps the discussions at the most productive levels. If I step too closely toward a book club and start asking questions that I think might lead the discussion in the "right" direction, I immediately see a decline in enthusiasm and passion for the topic. However, if I use this opportunity to grade a few papers, I emerge from my concentration on scoring a rubric to find that students have moved the discussion away from the book and onto a discussion about the plans for going to the movies after the Saturday soccer game.

It's all about the tight rope!

Students connect with text by discussing it.

The process for book club meetings is different from the process of strategy practice group meetings. With strategy practice groups, the process begins with the teacher providing guided instruction to small groups and continues with students practicing the skill and then writing about their strategy practice on the discussion board. With book clubs, the process is the exact opposite. The students begin to formulate ideas by collaborating on the discussion board, and then they meet face-to-face for discussions after they have been "playing" with ideas online. In the next chapter, you will see how this all fits together.

 Landry C. to ■ Out of My Mind (8th grade reading)
Please remember to bring your book and notes tomorrow to class. We will be discussing the differences between before and after Melanie receives her board.

The online classroom is a virtual meeting space where students prepare for face-to-face book club meetings.

Chapter Four Summary

▶ Each student is a part of two small groups: a strategy practice group and a book club. Blended learning occurs in each group since students meet with their groups face-to-face and online. You will learn about setting up an online discussion board in the next chapter.

▶ During the strategy practice group's face-to-face meetings, the teacher guides students through the practice of strategies that skilled readers use. Then, students practice those strategies online with group members by posting responses on the discussion board.

▶ Although fiction should not be abandoned, teachers should also provide informational texts for students to read since adults spend most of their reading time focused on this genre. Teachers have many online options from which to choose. Media specialists can direct teachers to the best sites or purchase subscriptions for teachers and students to use.

▶ As part of a book club, students participate in online discussions about a novel or nonfiction book. After they have played with ideas online, they meet face-to-face for a student-led discussion. The teacher acts as facilitator, interjecting only as needed.

Blended Strategies for Encouraging Students to Read and Reflect

The Discussion Board: A Tool for Strategy Practice Groups and Book Clubs

Just as you have set up places in the classroom where students will meet for guided strategy practice and for book clubs, you will also want to have places for members of groups to meet online. Writing about thinking offers students a chance to explore ideas and reflect on them in ways that will enrich face-to-face discussions. It also gives them a chance to move from "we do" to "you do."

A Student's Perspective

" I enjoy communicating online with my friends about what we are learning in school. "
—*Kate, intermediate student*

If your school district has a learning management system (LMS) such as one listed in Technology Tools for the Flipped Reading Block: An Annotated List of Resources (available online; see page 154 for details on how to access), by all means, use it. In this chapter, you will see screenshots from an Edmodo classroom. On an LMS like Edmodo, you can:

▸ Post your video-recorded mini-lessons

▸ Post links to articles, websites, or videos

▸ Create discussion boards on which small groups can communicate

▸ Give quizzes and assignments

▸ Collect assignments

If you do not have access to an LMS, you can set up your own discussion board on a wiki. Even a digital immigrant like me can set one up. Before using a learning management system, I created a wiki, and my students named it "Pasisis's Perspicacious Peeps." All the "peeps" in the class participated in discussions on different pages. The homepage began with the words, "We don't tweet; we peep."

> Go online to see a screencast tour of a sample Edmodo discussion board. See page 154 for details.

My students have always enjoyed activities that involve online social networking. Consider the popularity of Facebook, Twitter, and Instagram. Take advantage of that interest to lure your students into critical thinking, collaboration, communication, and creativity. You can hit all four 21st-century skills every time a student makes a hit on the discussion board!

Requiring that students write about reading is one of the keys to success that I have observed in teachers whose students make gains in literacy achievement. It not only provides an accountability measure, but it also forces students to practice active reading skills and to work on being metacognitive as they read.

One of the beauties of the discussion board is that virtual conversations are asynchronous, meaning that they can happen anywhere and at any time. You, as the teacher, create a "threaded discussion." The initial message on the "thread" includes a question or a prompt for the discussion. Then, students post their answers and respond to the answers of other students. The entire group of messages revolving around the prompt is the "thread."

A Student's Perspective

" I really like online discussions. The fact that I get to use a digital tool in class that I use daily outside of class makes me more interested in learning a topic. "

—Sarah, high-school student

> **Ethan T. to ◼ Slated (8th grade reading)**   ⌄
>
> Based on what you have read, what do you think will happen next? COMMENT BELOW
>
> ☺ ⌄   💬 7 Replies   ↗ Share   Nov 10, 2014
>
> **Aidan V.** said Nov 10, 2014
> She and her dad are going to fight
>
> **John Michael S.** said Nov 10, 2014
> I think she will be teased and bullied at school.
>
> **Nicolas B.** said Nov 10, 2014
> She won't be comfortable with her life. And something will happen.
>
> **Sarah M.** said Nov 10, 2014
> She won't like her new life
>
> **Kevin D.** said Nov 10, 2014
> I think she will be bullied or made made fun of at school.

Students can ask and answer questions on a discussion thread.

Threads for Strategy Practice Groups

Once you have created your strategy practice groups, you can begin threads for a variety of topics about which you wish students to write. The threads will align with your standards, flipped mini-lessons, whole-group guided practice, and small-group face-to-face practice.

Let's say you are teaching students to find a main idea in an informational article or excerpt from a book. Through a flipped lesson, you could explicitly teach students the strategy of looking for a common idea that appears in the beginning, the middle, and the end of an article or a passage from a story. You might even record your process of writing a post about the main idea before students write their own posts. That way, students can watch you compose a post that demonstrates your thinking as you use the beginning, middle, and end strategy to determine the main idea. Then, on the "main idea thread," students write about the main idea in the passage they read that day. Each student offers proof to support his or her claim about the main idea by supplying textual evidence and writing about how this idea appears throughout the text.

Main Idea   Assignment Options ⌄
Assignment Overview   All Submissions

Assigned to: ■ The Penguins (8th grade reading) , ■ The Turtles (8th grade reading)

Read the following article and determine the main idea.

More people are buying drones for fun, but they need to think of safety too
newsela.com

Megan K
Submitted on Dec 16, 2014 9:34 AM   [   ] / [   ]   Grade

In the article "More People Are Buying Drones for Fun, but They Need to Think of Safety too", the main idea was the safety of drones when in the hands of everyday people. In the article the author writes that drones are fun to play with, but can be considered a danger to many. The author states how many drones have been sold and how many are predicted to be sold. In the middle of the passage the author talks about the safety of airports and National Parks and how distracting the drones are. Because the idea of the drones' and others' safety was a topic in the beginning, middle, and end of the passage I know that is the main idea.

Let Megan K know what you thought of this submission…

😊 😊 😊 😐 😐 😊 😮 😟 😞

Screenshots of a prompt and response posted on an Edmodo LMS.

Using Writing Skeletons

Students may need help in structuring their writing, especially toward the beginning of the year. To help them, you might provide writing skeletons, or writing frames, for the skills you want them to reflect on through their posts.

Here is an example of a thread for a strategy group and a writing skeleton that students could use to post a response.

Thread Prompt:

Show the process you used to determine the main idea in the excerpt from *Bud, Not Buddy* (Curtis, 1999).

Skeleton:

> In the excerpt from [name the text], I determined the main idea. Throughout the passage, [write about the recurring idea]. [Give examples of the way the idea appears in the beginning, middle, and end of the passage.]

The students flesh out the skeleton by following the directions in the brackets. Here is a fleshed out skeleton:

> In the excerpt from *Bud, Not Buddy* (Curtis, 1999), I determined the main idea. Throughout the passage, the author, Curtis, writes that libraries have a hypnotizing smell. In the beginning of the passage, Curtis describes the smell of old books by using the adjectives "soft, drowsy, and powdery." In the middle of the passage, he describes how people fall asleep from the smell when the smelly powder weighs down eyelids. At the end, he writes about "tossing out drooly folks," who have been lured into a smell-induced sleep. Since the hypnotizing smell idea is in the beginning, middle, and end, I know it is the main idea.

In Appendix A, you will find a prompt for a thread, a writing skeleton, and a writing example to align with every strategy from the Chapter Three section, "What Skilled Readers Do" (see page 39). Some of the teachers I have coached have used these skeletons in their reading classrooms. The skeletons have been very helpful for students with writer's block at the beginning of the year. They give students a place to start and a structure for reflections of their reading experiences. I also have observed a fringe benefit that goes along with students using the skeletons as they learn to write about their application of strategies while reading—following the format of the skeletons improves student writing. Daily practice with these skeletons helps them learn how to introduce an idea and follow it with textual evidence that supports it. It also helps them learn to write introductory phrases and clauses and practice basic writing skills, such as how to place commas and quotation marks properly.

Although at first you might ask students to respond using the skeletons to help them learn how to reflect on their require of strategies during reading, it should be your goal to wean them off of the skeletons when they are ready. With daily writing practice, they will learn to write about reading without needing the skeletons. You can gradually release them from this structure as they develop their own authentic style.

Encouraging Students to Collaborate

Students do not just create one post for each of the threads; they also respond to each other's posts. I like to remind students that we are collaborating together, just as professionals do in the real world. Therefore, I encourage students to refer to one another as colleagues. A student responding to a colleague's intriguing word post might write about a different way of determining the meaning of the word or creatively use the word in an original sentence or poem. On another colleague's post on the question thread, the student could raise a new question or provide an answer to help a group member who experienced confusion during part of the reading. When students respond on a reading strategy thread, they may argue with each other: "I disagree with Julie, who made an inference that Bella's father has anger issues. I think his response shows fear for his daughter and a father's natural desire to protect his child." The discussion board provides a safe place to practice building on ideas, expressing differing opinions, and even disagreeing respectfully—all skills necessary for collaborating in the real world.

Using Posts as Assessments

Eric Jensen (2013) says that the best teachers "feast on data." They assess daily to gather data that can drive instruction. Although online posts are designed to support students in becoming metacognitive and thinking about their thinking, these posts can also provide you with rich information about where your students are in working toward goals and meeting the expectations set by the standards. You will be able to learn a great deal about whether or not students are successfully applying reading strategies or mastering skills by reading their posts. In this way, the posts can serve as a formative assessment.

If you are assessing students based on their posts, it is only fair that you are explicit in defining and communicating your expectations. Giving students a rubric is the best way for them to self-assess and continually set goals. Here are considerations for creating rubrics:

▶ What are the specific criteria?

▶ What is the evaluative range, with descriptions of characteristics of each specific level?

▶ What point system will you use if students earn grades based on the rubric?

When I create a rubric, I start by creating a table. After determining my criteria and evaluative range, I create columns and rows on the table. Then, I fill in the rubric with descriptions.

Consider, again, the response to this thread:

Show the process you used to determine the main idea in the excerpt from *Bud, Not Buddy*.

Here it is again:

In the excerpt from *Bud, Not Buddy* (Curtis, 1999), I determined the main idea. Throughout the passage, the author, Curtis, writes that libraries have a hypnotizing smell. In the beginning of the passage, Curtis describes the smell of old books by using the adjectives "soft, drowsy, and powdery." In the middle of the passage, he describes how people fall asleep from the smell when the smelly powder weighs down eyelids. At the end, he writes about "tossing out drooly folks," who have been lured into a smell-induced sleep. Since the hypnotizing smell idea is in the beginning, middle, and end, I know it is the main idea.

You could assess the skill of finding the main idea with a rubric. I always create rubrics that are student-friendly, and I ask students to self-assess before I assess them. The above example would earn a 3. It is substantive and on topic. The writer of the response captured the main idea.

0	1	2	3
I have not posted a response.	My post is brief and off topic. I have made only a minor attempt at explaining the process of finding my main idea.	My post is substantive and on topic. However, I have not fully explained the strategy I used for finding the main idea, and I am not certain what the main idea of the passage is.	My post is substantive and on topic. I have fully explained the strategy I used for finding the main idea, and I am certain that I have captured the main idea of the passage.

Again, a rubric not only helps you know which students need additional support, but it helps students as they set goals for themselves. You will learn more about the importance of goal-setting during reading instruction in Chapter Seven.

Threads for Book Clubs

The threads for the book clubs will be very different than those for the strategy practice groups because you want these discussions to be authentic—just like discussions in an adult book club that people join not because they have to join but because they want to.

In Chapter Four, you read about how to facilitate the setting up of deadlines and norms for your book clubs. Once a plan has been established, students are ready to begin an online discussion. Teachers who are successful in sparking rich discussions know that they must provide some type of structure in the beginning. Daniels and Steineke (2004) recommend that the teacher select a set of tasks for all the students in a book club to complete as they read. Doing so gives the students a focus during reading and something to talk about during online and face-to-face discussions. The tasks are specific, but students still maintain some decision-making as to the way they complete the tasks. Many teachers have used this strategy successfully in preparation for face-to-face discussions, and you can apply this strategy if your students need structure in the beginning of their online book discussions.

I have adapted the idea of specific tasks into a menu of online discussion options in the form of thread prompts. Since we can be certain that students are focusing on targeted, teacher-selected skills in strategy practice groups, we can afford to loosen the reins and empower students to exert more control during book clubs.

I will share with you a menu of discussion thread ideas that provide many ways readers may wish to interact with text and talk about it in an online format. Of course, you may wish to adapt these ideas and add additional ideas of your own. Once students practice responding to your prompts, you might allow them to create the prompts for the threaded discussions; you can see an example of a student-created prompt on page 62.

> ➤ An important thread is the "connections thread." Remember that skilled readers continually make connections as they read. Students might write about personal connections or interdisciplinary connections to social studies, science, math, or art. They might also make connections to other texts, current events, music, movies, theater, sports, or anything else that might provide fellow group members with a deeper understanding of the text. Students can even add links to websites and articles for their group members to read.

Mrs. Morgan to ■ Out of My Mind (8th grade reading)

Connections - Is there something you can share here that might help fellow group members understand this novel better? A personal connection? Something from history or current events that this reminds you of? Please feel free to add links to websites and articles if you wish.

☺ ∨ · Q 5 Replies · ⌃ Share   Oct 29, 2014

Show more replies...

Zoe W. said Dec 16, 2014
I went to Barnes and Nobles, with my good friend Abby S. and another friend. There was this girl who was about Melody's age in a wheelchair. There were some kids there who were making fun of her because she couldn't control her actions. That really upset me.

Landry C. said Dec 16, 2014
About a week ago, I was watching the news on T.V. The anchors were talking about a family whom had a child with cerebral palsy who claimed the airline humiliated them while on a flight. They were demanding an apology from the airline and the stewardess. It broke my heart to see how they were treated.

Jared C. said Dec 16, 2014
In this book, I feel like Melody went through some of the same problems unpopular students did with the poor treatment. Hers was much worse because she had no ability to communicate how much she was hurt. I wonder how much some people automatically assume handicapped people are 'dumb' just because of their inability to communicate.

Making connections can help students understand a text more deeply.

Menu of Discussion Threads for Book Clubs

Connections

Visuals

Questions

Predictions

Powerful Excerpts

Literary Elements

Interesting Words

Thinking

► "Visuals" could be a very engaging thread, especially with the popularity of graphic novels. On this thread, students could post images related to the reading. If the book takes place during a different historical period, students could find pictures that show how people dressed during the period or what their transportation looked like. They might use apps to create cartoons in order to add a graphic novel feature to a book containing no pictures. (You can find tools for these activities in Technology Tools for the Flipped Reading Block: An Annotated List of Resources, available online; see page 154 for details on how to access.) If the book takes place in a different country, they might post pictures or videos of that part of the world. They could even draw pictures using an online drawing tool.

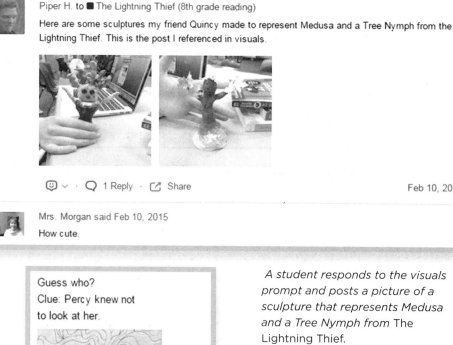

Mrs. Morgan to ■ The Lightning Thief (8th grade reading)

Visual - Are you a visual learner? Are your fellow readers? Here is a great place to post images related to the novel. You can also create cartoons to add a graphic novel feel to the book. You can draw your own images of what you think the characters look like.

Piper H. to ■ The Lightning Thief (8th grade reading)

Here are some sculptures my friend Quincy made to represent Medusa and a Tree Nymph from the Lightning Thief. This is the post I referenced in visuals.

☺ ∨ · ◯ 1 Reply · ⤴ Share   Feb 10, 2015

Mrs. Morgan said Feb 10, 2015
How cute.

A student responds to the visuals prompt and posts a picture of a sculpture that represents Medusa and a Tree Nymph from The Lightning Thief.

Guess who?
Clue: Percy knew not to look at her.

☺ ∨ · ◯ Reply · ⤴ Share

A student posts a drawing of Medusa from The Lightning Thief.

Student cartoon in reaction to Island of Hope: The Story of Ellis Island and the Journey to America *by Martin Sandler, posted to the Visuals thread.*

➤ The "question thread" is an important one, since I have observed that students ask very few questions in many of the classrooms I visit. On this thread, students can post questions inspired by the text. They may also ask questions about parts of the story that confused them. Students can work collaboratively to answer each other's questions. A student might raise another question in response to a post or might provide an answer to another student who experienced confusion during part of the reading. As students read each other's questions, they witness how other students think and interact with text. This helps passive readers see what it looks like to be an active reader.

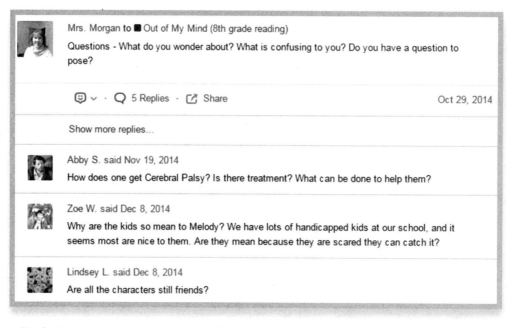

Students post questions and respond to each other's questions on the Question thread.

➤ On the "predictions," or "prophecy," thread, students can post predictions and write about the textual evidence they used to make those predictions.

> **Mrs. Morgan to ■ Out of My Mind (8th grade reading)**
>
> Prophecy - What are your predictions? Show evidence from the text to support your hypothesis. Check back later to see if you were right.
>
> 🙂 ⌄ · 💬 6 Replies · ⎘ Share   Oct 29, 2014
>
> Show more replies...
>
> **Abby S. said Nov 4, 2014**
> The book will most likely be sad, seeing that it's about a girl with a handicap. Even though I'm drawn to thinking the book is about a goldfish, most likely it is not.Someone who might have been kidnapped or captured, or possibly just looking for themselves.
>
> **Zoe W. said Nov 19, 2014**
> I think our predictions were pretty close.
>
> **Abby S. said Dec 8, 2014**
> After reading the book I realize that the fish bowl is in the story, but it is also a metaphor for her life.

Students make predictions and reflect on them in this thread.

➤ "Powerful excerpts" could be a thread of discussion posts on which students write quotes from the text that are significant, well-crafted, or emotionally charged. The student can explain why each quote has special meaning.

> **Mrs. Morgan to ■ Out of My Mind (8th grade reading)**
> Powerful Excerpts - Share book quotes that are significant, well-crafted, or emotionally charged. Tell why these quotes have a special meaning to you.
>
> 🙂 ⌄ · 💬 3 Replies · ⎘ Share   Oct 29, 2014
>
> **Abby S. said Nov 19, 2014**
> "A person is much more than the name of a diagnosis on a chart." I feel this is so true. So many people look at how you dress, or speak, and make a snap judgement about you. We are all more than the surface.
>
> **Zoe W. said Nov 19, 2014**
> "We all have disabilities. What's yours?"
>
> **Jared C. said Dec 8, 2014**
> "It's like I've been given a bunch of puzzle pieces without the picture on the cover of the box to go by."
> I think we all feel like this sometimes, but for us, the cover eventually shows up. It never did for Melody.

Students share favorite quotes from the text and discuss why each is important.

➤ The "literary element thread" will encourage students to examine an author's techniques and show how the author's craft makes the writing rich.

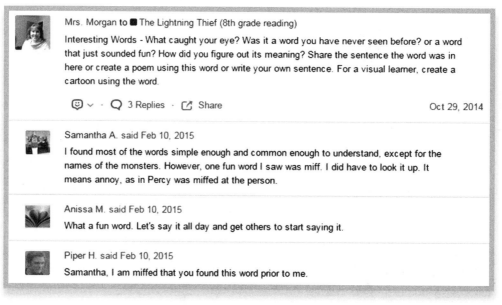

Mrs. Morgan to ■ Out of My Mind (8th grade reading)

Literary Elements - Examine the author's techniques and show how the use of his craft makes the writing rich.

☺ ∨ · Q 3 Replies · ⤢ Share   Oct 29, 2014

Abby S. said Nov 7, 2014

I'd never read any Sharon Draper books, and I was quite surprised situation she addressed. I'm wanting to read more by here now.

Landry C. said Nov 14, 2014

Sharon Draper uses techniques that don't give away the plot until the very end. She uses show and not tell. She is also very descriptive when developing characters. You feel as if you know the characters personally.

Lindsey L. said Dec 8, 2014

I love Sharon Draper because she makes the book very relatable in that all the situations she puts into the book could really happen.

Students explore literary elements on this thread.

▶ "Interesting words" is a thread every group should have. Like they do in their strategy practice groups, students in book clubs will post words. However, while they must follow a specific procedure in their strategy practice groups, they will have more freedom in their book club to write whatever they wish to write about the interesting word they found. They may wish to write the sentence in which it was found or an explanation of their process for figuring out the word's meaning. Or they may want to use the word in a sentence or short poem of their own, or use an online tool to create a cartoon using the word.

Mrs. Morgan to ■ The Lightning Thief (8th grade reading)

Interesting Words - What caught your eye? Was it a word you have never seen before? or a word that just sounded fun? How did you figure out its meaning? Share the sentence the word was in here or create a poem using this word or write your own sentence. For a visual learner, create a cartoon using the word.

☺ ∨ · Q 3 Replies · ⤢ Share   Oct 29, 2014

Samantha A. said Feb 10, 2015

I found most of the words simple enough and common enough to understand, except for the names of the monsters. However, one fun word I saw was miff. I did have to look it up. It means annoy, as in Percy was miffed at the person.

Anissa M. said Feb 10, 2015

What a fun word. Let's say it all day and get others to start saying it.

Piper H. said Feb 10, 2015

Samantha, I am miffed that you found this word prior to me.

Students share interesting words on this thread.

▶ "Characters" is a thread that students enjoy. On this thread, students can be psychologists who analyze characters and support their analyses with evidence. My experience is that this thread will be a popular one for online debates; and as long as students are respectful, I would encourage these arguments, since they push students to think critically.

Students analyze and discuss character traits, motivations, actions, and decisions on this thread.

▶ Finally, the "thinking thread" will be a place for each reader to post life lessons learned from the book. This will be a place in which students will explore what it means to be human. This thread will likely be one that inspires topics for face-to-face discussions.

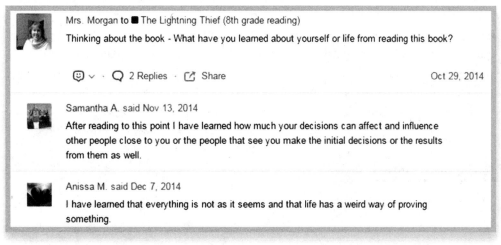

Students explore themes and big ideas on the Thinking thread.

Students have many choices, so they should not have to be a part of each threaded discussion. As they read, they can decide on which threads they wish to post. This will make the discussions genuine. Again, as discussion leaders create a deadlines and norms plan, they decide how many times a week students in the book club should post on the discussion board. We want students to post often enough to stay connected, but not so often that the posting responsibility becomes burdensome rather than reflective and inspiring. Requiring two to five posts a week generally seems to work well to maintain that balance. More than five seems excessive, especially since students also have the responsibility of posting as part of strategy practice group members.

> ## A Student's Perspective
>
> " Effective teachers find out how their students learn most effectively and give them the chance to learn that way. "
> —*Michael, high-school student*

When Do Students Post on the Discussion Board, and What Does This Time Look Like?

At the beginning of the year, you need to model how to post. You will show students how to use the discussion board and how to access it both in the classroom and remotely. You will also show them what a quality post looks like. You might project your own responses to literature as well as examples of high-quality student responses. You could show a student response and then ask students to discuss it. "Why do you think this response represents insight?"

If you decide to show examples of poor responses, make sure to show responses that have *not* been written by your students. Intentionally write an inadequate response yourself, and let students analyze it and talk about what makes it inadequate. Reassure your students that you would never highlight an actual student's response for its weakness. Let them know that you will only highlight responses that show strength in some area. Sadly, I watched a teacher harshly critique a student's writing in front of the class, and I saw how this stunted the student's literacy growth because the student shut down completely. This kind of action can also make students in general hesitate to share or take risks.

While you should certainly allow students to post on the discussion board outside of class, you should also provide in-class time for writing. This can look different in each teacher's classroom. If you are fortunate enough to be in a classroom equipped with a full set of tablets or laptops, then you may have

> ## A Student's Perspective
>
> " The teacher needs to be precise in instructions. I like a set of rules as a foundation even though I want to let my ideas roam free. "
> —*Helen, high-school student*

all students writing at the same time, with the exception of the small group with whom you are providing small-group instruction. If you do not have the luxury of a classroom set of devices, you may have your classroom set up in stations. The next section will provide examples of what this might look like.

It is imperative that you train students in what their behavior should look like during online response time. From the very first day, you must help them acquire the necessary writing behavior to make them successful in their response to reading time. Here are writing behaviors you should expect and teach:

▶ **Staying quiet:** Response time should be absolutely quiet so that students can think. Chatter from others can disturb the thought process and cause a student to disengage from the hard work involved in making sense of text. Voices must be off at this time.

▶ **Staying still:** Moving around can cause the same disengagement. Although I encourage movement at other times, during this part of the reading block, students must learn to sit without moving around. Their typing fingers should be the only body part moving. During their time on the discussion board, students should toggle back and forth between the discussion board and the text to which they are responding.

▶ **Staying focused:** Students should not be visiting other websites unless they are finding images or related readings to post on the discussion board. You can monitor students on your own screen with an online management program that allows you to see all screens. You will find examples of such programs in Technology Tools for the Flipped Reading Block: An Annotated List of Resources, available online; see page 154 for details on how to access.

To train students in these essential behaviors, you might post the expected behaviors on the wall. Boushey and Moser (2006) recommend asking students to model behaviors you wish for them to practice. They also recommend that you model what this time should *not* look like. It may take repeated modeling for students to really understand the expectations, but that is okay. It takes time to firmly establish habits.

To reinforce positive behavior and discourage undesirable behavior, you might require students to self-assess on a response to writing rubric. Here is an example:

0	1	2	3
My writing time was unproductive because I did not stay focused on the task.	I was only productive part of the time, and I required teacher redirection to stay on task.	I stayed focused and was productive most of the time.	I was highly productive because I wrote during the entire reading response time without talking or leaving my seat for any reason.

You need to continue to monitor students with hyper-vigilance until they establish independent behaviors. You will not begin working in small groups for more than a few minutes at a time until good habits are firmly planted. Once the behaviors become habits, though, you will want to use this time, while students are working independently, to pull aside small groups. When my students established positive learning habits and did not require my redirection, I was tempted to use this quiet time for checking my e-mail and lesson planning, but I had to resist the temptation. I knew that students needed this time to work in small groups with me. In my observations, the teachers whose students grew in reading (with a side benefit of increased test scores) used almost every minute of student independent reading and writing time to work strategically with small groups.

A Student's Perspective

" Teachers should not pay attention to their computers all day and ignore their students.
—*Dean, middle-school student* "

What If a Classroom Does Not Have a Full Set of Devices?

If your school does not have a 1:1 initiative, and you do not have a classroom set of devices, you will need to be creative, but you can still employ a discussion board to assist students in reflecting on and monitoring their learning. Here are some ideas.

BYOD (Bring Your Own Device)

Ask your principal if you can allow students to bring in their own devices. Many of the learning management systems can be accessed on smartphones and tablets.

The difficulty comes when a few students show up without a device. If you have any computers in your classroom, these students could use them while the others are working on their own devices.

Tablet or Computer Carts

Many schools that have not initiated a 1:1 program have computer carts that can be checked out. Sign up for these as often as you can! Let's say you can check them out two days a week—on those days, you will want to give students a longer period of time to work on the discussion board. Limit the reading time accordingly and provide extra reading minutes on the other days. On the days when you do not have the computers, students can jot down their ideas on sticky notes. Then, they can refer to these ideas and synthesize them on the days on which they have access to the discussion board.

A Set of Computers Housed in the Classroom

If you have a limited set of computers in your classroom, you may need to create a rotation routine, or stations. Instead of having all of the students reading at one time and all of the students writing at one time, you might need to have one group working on the computers while others are reading or working on another task. Here is how a sample of your rotation schedule might look in a 58-minute reading block:

Group A:

8:52–8:58:	Whole-class follow-up to the flipped lesson (including partner activities)
9:00–9:13:	Computer time—writing on discussion board
9:15–9:28:	Strategy practice group with the teacher
9:30–9:45:	Reading
9:45–9:50:	Whole-class closure

Group B:

8:52–8:58:	Whole-class follow-up to the flipped lesson (including partner activities)
9:00–9:13:	Reading
9:15–9:28:	Computer time—writing on discussion board
9:30–9:45:	Strategy practice group with the teacher
9:45–9:50:	Whole-class closure

Group C:

8:52–8:58:	Whole-class follow-up to the flipped lesson (including partner activities)
9:00–9:13:	Strategy practice group with the teacher
9:15–9:30:	Reading
9:32–9:45:	Computer time—writing on discussion board
9:45–9:50:	Whole-class closure

Incorporating Face-to-Face Discussions

In addition to time spent engaging in follow-up to the mini-lesson activities, reading, writing about reading on discussion boards, and working with the teacher in guided strategy practice groups, students also need face-to-face time to talk with other students.

You might devote time during one or two class periods per week for students to talk face-to-face in their book clubs. For these meetings, you could ask students to take turns being the discussion leader. Here are possible duties to assign to the discussion leader:

▶ **Plan Topics:** The leader reads the posts on the discussion board and uses them to plan topics for discussion. For instance, if there were multiple posts that signaled that a part of a passage was confusing, the discussion leader might ask the others in the group to provide clarification or strategies for figuring it out. One student might say, "The second and third paragraphs were really confusing, so I read them over again and wrote the main ideas of each paragraph in the margin."

▶ **Ask a Debatable Question:** The discussion leader could also ask a debatable question, like: "In this informational passage about the Battle of Little Bighorn, do you think Custer was brave or just impulsive?" One student might answer, "When I read about how Custer made the decision to charge before really assessing the situation, I made an inference that he was impulsive." Another student might say, "I think he was brave because he did not have time to assess the situation, so he decided to act offensively."

▶ **Focus the Discussion on Writer's Craft:** The leader may ask colleagues to read aloud a passage that was posted on the discussion board. Then, the group can analyze symbols used in the passage or show how an author effectively uses a literary element such as metaphor.

▶ **Hold Group Members Accountable:** The leader may review norms and act as a guide who redirects students who are not meeting the norms by giving gentle reminders.

As students learn how to read actively and think about what they are reading, you can encourage them to move their discussions into higher realms of thinking. This may involve meeting with the discussion leader to support him or her in writing questions that will provoke depth of thought. Students might evaluate actions of the characters or connect the ideas from their book to larger societal issues. You could even assess discussion leaders on the questions they ask their group by referring to Bloom's Taxonomy (Anderson, Airasian, Cruikshank, Mayer, Pintrich, Raths, & Wittrock, 2001). Evaluative questions earn high values, while the values of summarization questions are low. The leader might give all group members a copy of Bloom's Taxonomy and ask them to circle the thinking levels of their responses. Providing this type of feedback is another way to help students learn to write questions and deliver responses that will inspire rich discussions.

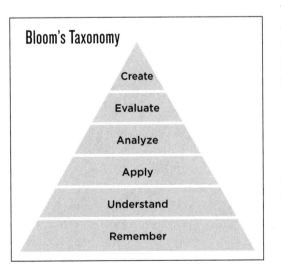

Bloom's Taxonomy

- Create
- Evaluate
- Analyze
- Apply
- Understand
- Remember

I have witnessed what happens when students participate in these types of critical thinking discussions. By questioning and listening to the perspectives of others as well as expressing their own ideas, students explore what they consider to be right and wrong. Each student builds his or her unique belief system, grows in the ability to look at situations from multiple perspectives, and develops empathy. In my observations, this highly engaging type of thinking excites students and makes them want to read and think more.

Remember, you want students to be metacognitive as they participate in discussions. Rubrics are the perfect tool for that. Here is an example rubric that you might have students use during book club meetings:

0	1	2	3
I showed little control over my voice or body and disrupted the group with inappropriate interruptions.	I listened respectfully but did not make substantive contributions to the discussion.	I actively participated with substantive contributions, but not all of my comments were backed with textual evidence.	I actively participated in a respectful and appropriate manner, and my contributions to the discussion were insightful and backed with textual evidence.

Students will, of course, have the opportunity to be metacognitive in their book clubs, but those face-to-face meetings may only occur once or twice a week. In between those meetings, we need to give students additional times to talk, even if we don't have time for an extended discussion.

Maintaining Reading Time

While students work on building skills, they must spend time reading and reflecting on their reading. This is the "you do" of "I do; we do; you do." There are times when the classroom needs to be very quiet in order to allow this skill building to happen. Students can sustain this quiet practice if we give them talking breaks.

If you punctuate quiet time with short bursts of talking time, students will be better able to stay focused when you need them to read and write quietly. As I demonstrated in Chapter Three, you can energize your follow-up to flipped mini-lessons with partner activities. You might also give students a chance to talk in short spurts as they work with their strategy practice groups, even when you are not facilitating those groups. For instance, as a follow-up to your guided practice, you might provide students with a face-to-face, collaborative activity during which they work on words. Focusing on a specific root word, students could work together on a word scavenger hunt in the articles they are reading. Or you could divide an article into sections and ask the members of a strategy practice group to work together to create a seven-word summary of each section. Activities that allow students to talk to one another will complement the online activities as well as the silent reading and reflecting time, all of which are necessary for students to grow as readers.

Collaborative and Independent Projects

While students are reading, or after they have finished reading, encourage holistic reflection. With choice-driven projects that interest students, this can be an exciting time for students to synthesize their learning, reflect on what they have read, and work (independently or collaboratively) on a creative project that shows and celebrates their reading accomplishments. They may work on the project during the time designed for group online and face-to-face discussions. Since students practice collective innovation as they work on the project, they can use an online tool for communication. You can find online tools for this type of collaboration in Technology Tools for the Flipped Reading Block: An Annotated List of Resources, available online; see page 154 for details on how to access. Blended collaboration is what happens in the modern adult world, so students will benefit from practicing it while they are in school.

> ## A Student's Perspective
>
> " An effective teacher plans interactive projects with a twist to make learning fun.
> —*Elizabeth, middle-school student* "

Below you will find some ideas for projects. Do not limit yourself to this list. Let this list and your ideas spark the creativity of your students, who will likely come up with their own ideas, too. This is a time when choice can motivate learners. Many of these project ideas can be completed using low- or high-tech tools. In Technology Tools for the Flipped Reading Block, you will find descriptions and online addresses of technology tools that can support students in these projects, such as book creators, video creation tools, digital art tools, visual organizers, game creators, cartoon creators, note-taking apps, presentation tools, and more. Keep in mind that new technology resources are constantly being developed, so explore the most current apps and find a tool that will provide students with the best possible experience.

Notice how many of the projects allow students to use both words and visuals. For contemporary learners, visual literacy is an important skill.

▶ Write a scene for a screenplay based on a book.

▶ Write and illustrate a pop-up book to retell a story. (Explore the online book creators in Technology Tools for the Flipped Reading Block: An Annotated List of Resources for digital options.)

- Turn part of a novel into a children's book that includes words and illustrations. (Explore the online book creators in Technology Tools for the Flipped Reading Block for digital options.)

- Produce a book trailer. (Explore the video creation tools in Technology Tools for the Flipped Reading Block for digital options.)

- Create a painting that depicts a setting. Use acrylics, watercolors, or oils. (Explore the digital art tools in Technology Tools for the Flipped Reading Block for digital options.)

- Write a newspaper clipping that relates to a novel. (Explore the digital news story creators in Technology Tools for the Flipped Reading Block for digital options.)

- Design a brochure inviting people to come to the town in which a novel is set. (Explore the online booklet creators in Technology Tools for the Flipped Reading Block for digital options.)

- Visually organize ideas related to the parts of a book. (Explore the digital visual organizers in Technology Tools for the Flipped Reading Block for digital options.)

- Create a speaking avatar to show characterization. (Explore the avatar creators in Technology Tools for the Flipped Reading Block for digital options.)

- Paint a mural with images relating to a book and the author's themes.

- Connect ideas in a book to a historical context and write a research paper.

- Develop a timeline to depict the parts of a novel. (Explore the digital visual organizers in Technology Tools for the Flipped Reading Block for digital options.)

- Use a template to create a fake Facebook page and then post the page on the discussion board.

- Design a video game based on ideas in a book. (Explore the game creators in Technology Tools for the Flipped Reading Block for digital options.)

- Write a poem, rap, or song based on ideas from a book.

- Write and illustrate part of a book as a chapter in a graphic novel. (Explore cartoon creators in Technology Tools for the Flipped Reading Block for digital options.)

- Write and illustrate a cartoon based on part of a book. (Explore cartoon creators in Technology Tools for the Flipped Reading Block for digital options.)

- Create an online, interactive poster or collage. (Explore digital poster

> Technology Tools for the Flipped Reading Block: An Annotated List of Resources is available online; see page 154 for details on how to access.

and collage creators in Technology Tools for the Flipped Reading Block for digital options.)

- ▶ Design a photo story about part of a book. (Explore storytelling tools in Technology Tools for the Flipped Reading Block for digital options.)

- ▶ Write and illustrate a journal. (Explore note-taking apps in Technology Tools for the Flipped Reading Block for digital options.)

- ▶ Create and teach a lesson that shows how to develop a specific reading skill. (Explore presentation tools and screencast makers in Technology Tools for the Flipped Reading Block for digital options.)

- ▶ Compare and contrast two characters with both words and images. (Explore digital visual organizers in Technology Tools for the Flipped Reading Block for digital options.)

- ▶ Combine links, videos, and photos related to the theme of a book. (Explore content curation tools in Technology Tools for the Flipped Reading Block for digital options.)

- ▶ Sketch the setting or characters. (Explore digital art tools in Technology Tools for the Flipped Reading Block for digital options.)

- ▶ Illustrate a scene from a book. (Explore digital art tools in Technology Tools for the Flipped Reading Block for digital options.)

- ▶ Create a Venn diagram that compares and contrasts characters or themes. (Explore digital visual organizers in Technology Tools for the Flipped Reading Block for options.)

- ▶ Create visually appealing postcards that characters might write to one another. (Explore note-taking apps in Technology Tools for the Flipped Reading Block for digital options.)

- ▶ Summarize a novel by creating an animated flipbook. (Explore digital flipbook and cartoon creators in Technology Tools for the Flipped Reading Block for digital options.)

- ▶ Create a movie based on a novel. (Explore video creation tools in Technology Tools for the Flipped Reading Block.)

- ▶ Write an illustrated short story based on one of the themes from a book. (Explore online book creators in Technology Tools for the Flipped Reading Block for digital options.)

- ▶ Compile information related to an author (links to articles, YouTube clips, author's website, etc.). (Explore content curation tools in Technology Tools for the Flipped Reading Block for digital options.)

- ▶ Tell about the history on which a novel is based. (Explore storytelling tools in Technology Tools for the Flipped Reading Block for digital options.)

- ▶ Choreograph a dance based on a story.

 The Flipped Reading Block © 2015 by Gina Pasisis, Scholastic Teaching Resources

- ▶ Write a song or a musical based on the book. (Explore sound recording tools in Technology Tools for the Flipped Reading Block for digital options.)

- ▶ Create a song from a montage of inspirational quotes from the book and/ or quotes and ideas from other sources that have a similar theme. (Explore sound recording tools in Technology Tools for the Flipped Reading Block for digital options.)

- ▶ Create a 3-D model of the setting.

- ▶ Make a scrapbook for a character.

Students create a scrapbook for a character.

Although students may spend some time working on these projects online, they will also need face-to-face time as they create. Be sure to put procedures in place so that this active learning does not leave you with a pounding headache at the end of the day.

Students collaborate on ideas for reflective projects.

Students build a model of the setting.

A Student's Perspective

" A characteristic of an effective teacher is an ability to control the classroom, but at the same time make it fun so that it isn't boring.
—*Joe, middle-school student* "

My experience has taught me that students get very excited during collective innovation, and this can result in loud, enthusiastic voices. If students begin group work already talking in loud tones, the noise level will grow and grow as everyone tries to speak over each other.

Therefore, it is essential that you work with your students on "low talking" during the first weeks of school. It takes about three weeks for students to establish habits, but once they get into the habit of speaking in low tones, they will do it without even thinking about it for the rest of the school year. I create cards that read "way too loud," "too loud," and "just right." Then, I walk around the room and flash the appropriate card at each group. For the first few weeks, I give a reward to the group that stays at "just right" for the longest period of time during collaborative work. The reward can be simple; I might say, for instance, "The group that stays at 'just right' for the longest period gets first choice in selecting spots during silent reading today." You may be surprised at how quickly students learn to speak in just above whisper tones if you spend a little time training them. Low talking is one of the most powerful lessons you teach, for it will let you have a very active classroom that does not leave you exhausted at the end of the day. Students also enjoy the experience of active learning that is not deafening!

In addition to managing noise level, here are some other procedures to consider:

▶ **Supplies:** Have a system for storing supplies and make groups responsible for keeping their work areas tidy.

- **Movement:** Make a plan for students to move to specific locations in the classroom.
- **Devices:** Create a check-out schedule so that all groups have fair and equitable access to any technology.

Of course, the projects provide you with another opportunity to assess learning. Since this project is open-ended, you may wish to ask book clubs or individuals to create their own rubrics to align with their project ideas. You could inform them of key components that you want them to self-assess. For instance, you may ask them to include a section on positive, collaborative work habits, such as staying on task, treating team members with respect, and equitably dividing tasks among members. You might also ask them to include a section on whether or not the final project shows students' understanding of characterization, theme, inferences, or whatever skill was the focus for this particular project. I have found that the quality of student projects is higher when students design their self-assessments.

Chapter Five Summary

- The discussion board can be a tool for learner reflection, and it can be the component of online learning that leads to higher engagement and achievement.

- Students should be members of both a strategy practice group and an online book club on the discussion board.

- The teacher can create "threaded discussions" that include an initial prompt for discussion. Then, students post responses to the prompt and responses to the posts made by their colleagues. The entire group of messages revolving around the prompt is called a "thread."

- The teacher must train students on the learning behaviors they must practice during reading response time so that all students can enter the thinking realm.

- Student book club leaders can use content from the online discussions to create questions for rich, face-to-face discussions.

- Teachers can encourage holistic reflection of a text through independent or collaborative projects.

- Using rubrics, teachers can use discussion board posts and collaborative projects to assess learning.

Eyes on Text: A Simple Solution to Our Nation's Reading Crisis

A Case for Daily Reading

You might say that I did a little study of my own. Having raised two children, I will own up to the fact that I did not always enforce the at-home reading that teachers required. I regret to admit it, especially since I am a reading teacher and I know the importance of reading for academic success in all subject areas. It's just that we often ran out of time. After baseball practice, ballet lessons, and homework, we had a choice: stay up until midnight and read or try to get at least a percentage of the recommended amount of sleep.

This is not just my story. I have many friends who were my fellow baseball-and-ballet moms. They had the same problem. We made sure our children completed the assignments that had to be turned in for a grade, but ran out of time when it came to supervising our children in doing what matters most: reading.

Wider research supports that this story extends well beyond my community. Americans between the ages of 15 and 24 spend an average of seven minutes a day reading, and only one-third of 13-year-olds are daily readers (Gallagher, 2009, p. 41).

Some may say that those who advocate for the resurrection of Sustained Silent Reading (SSR), which has been dropped by some schools, are giving up on parents, but I disagree. I believe parents have the best intentions. They simply run out of time. That's my story, and I am sticking to it!

The fact is, students are not reading at home, and yet we know that time spent with eyes on text predicts achievement. Just look at the following chart for proof.

Average Reading Scores by Frequency of Reading for Fun

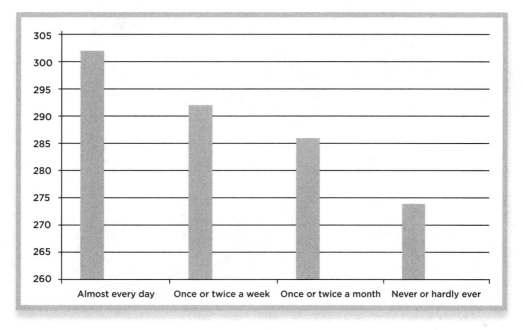

(U.S. Department of Education Statistics, cited in Gallagher, 2009, p. 36)

Being part of a community of readers seems to encourage the habit of reading for pleasure. Teens, especially, report that they enjoy reading alongside other teens and they are especially motivated by the prospect of talking to their friends about what they are reading (Howard, 2009).

The biggest argument against traditional SSR philosophy is that some students simply will not read when given the opportunity to read for pleasure unless there is added accountability. In fact, a study by Debra Von Sprecken and Stephen Krashen found that 90% of students observed actually do read during SSR (Krashen, 2004).

Enter the discussion board. While my students tend to shut down when faced with a worksheet, they welcome the opportunity to participate on the discussion board. Aren't convinced students like to share their ideas online with one another? Ask them how many of them tweet.

In short, time to read for pleasure + time to talk to friends about reading on a discussion board = reading class nirvana.

Just because teachers give students time to read in class does not mean that out-of-class reading assignments should cease. If a student gets hooked on a book in class, logic tells me that there is a greater likelihood he or she will continue to read after the school bell rings. Also, if students have a part in setting their own goals about reading, and if students find accountability from a community of peers in online and face-to-face, student-led discussions, the likelihood of completion of at-home reading assignments just might be greater.

A student reads independently in a comfortable classroom spot of her choosing.

Building Reading Endurance

It is clear from the research that having eyes on text leads to improvement in literacy. Research also tells us that we should ensure that students are actually reading when we give them time in class to read. For the bibliophiles in the classroom, this is not a problem because these students love books and read whenever they have the chance. They may, from time to time, *steal* the chance when they are supposed to be working on math problems or listening to lectures. Ironically, these students often get in trouble for reading. You can see these students absolutely devouring books during the individual reading segment of the literacy block. Because they are natural lovers of literature, these students would grow as readers if they were merely placed in a room with a stack of books—even if you took a trip to the Bahamas and forgot to contact a substitute!

However, the problem with periods of sustained silent reading is that struggling and reluctant readers find ways to *pretend* they are reading when they actually are not. Often, these readers have had nothing but painful experiences with reading, so when the teacher uses the acronym SSR, the struggling readers hear "anesthesia." If individually selected novels are the only texts students are reading during a literacy block, then the teacher cannot really hold students accountable for reading. As I visit classrooms in my role as an instructional coach, I observe students during silent reading activities. I find, as Krashen observed, that most students are actually reading. However, I notice that some students who are sitting quietly and appear to be reading, are really just staring at the pages as if in a trance. The passively compliant students often go unnoticed until test scores show that they have failed to grow in reading achievement.

> ### A Student's Perspective
>
> 66 It is kind of blissful when the teacher gives us time to read in class.
> —*Maria, middle-school student* 99

How, then, do you ensure that students are reading actively during this silent reading time? Accountability is the key. With the blended approach I am suggesting, students have layers of accountability for reading. They are accountable to their teacher both online and face-to-face as part of their strategy practice groups. They are accountable to their peers both online and face-to-face as part of their book clubs. As you will learn in the next chapter, they are also accountable to themselves because they will set long-term and short-term goals, and continually self-assess their progress toward those goals.

Accountability is what encourages students to read initially, but effective teachers create an environment that makes reading pleasurable so that, eventually, students read because they enjoy the experience.

Making the classroom comfortable is one way to make silent reading enjoyable. I would suggest investing in some big pillows, bean bag chairs, and a rug. During quiet reading time, I allow students to find cozy places throughout the room. Students may sit on the floor or in their seats. To be fair to all, you can dismiss students in sections, dismissing a different section first each day. That way, every student will have a shot at the prime spots. Even eighth graders, your oldest middle school students, enjoy this opportunity to move from their desks to find a relaxing place to read.

> ### A Student's Perspective
>
> 66 I can read longer if I don't have to sit at a hard desk the whole time.
> —*Danny, middle-school student* 99

For this quiet reading time to work, you must spend a considerable amount of time at the beginning of the year teaching students to develop the stamina for sitting still and focusing intensely for a period of time. The first few weeks of school are the prime opportunity for supporting students as they work toward endurance for independent reading. During these weeks, you can record data on rubrics to assess students on their ability to sit still and stay focused on reading without talking or bothering others. You may want to pull an individual student or a few students for a short spurt of instruction, but it is not the moment yet to devote a long period of time to a small-group lesson. Students must get into the habit of reading without becoming distracted before you can divert your focus from your quiet, unobtrusive support of those positive habits. Every class will be different, but students in the intermediate and middle grades may only be able to stay focused for five to ten minutes at the beginning of the year. With practice, students can increase that time, and by the end of the first three weeks, students should be able to stay focused for 20 to 30 minutes.

During this training period, students can self-assess to set their own goals for increasing their endurance. Once they have trained themselves to do this, you will no longer need to monitor them so closely. They will begin to enjoy having this time to surrender completely to a good book. Here is a sample rubric you can have students use to self-assess as they work to meet expectations during reading time:

0	I	2	3
I did not stay focused on reading during reading time.	I stayed focused some of the time but needed some redirection from my teacher.	I stayed focused most of the time, and when I did become distracted, I was able to redirect myself.	I stayed intensely focused on reading for the entire reading time.

Students enjoy reading in comfortable spots that they select.

Fostering Active Engagement

In addition to teaching students how to stay focused on text, you will want to encourage students to practice active reading strategies. During the period of silent reading, students will learn to interact with text and master reading skills. While students read, they should annotate the text. Here are some ideas for annotating:

- ▶ Underline or highlight interesting words, phrases, figurative language, and insightful quotes.

- ▶ Underline or highlight ideas essential to understanding the big ideas in the text.

- ▶ Write notes in the margin to make connections with text and express thoughts about an event or decision made by a character (in fiction) or a person (in nonfiction).

- ▶ Write notes in the margin (or on sticky notes) when making an inference or prediction.

- ▶ Highlight unknown words and the context clues that assist in determining word meaning.

- ▶ Put a question mark by a confusing piece of text. Then, go back, reread, and underline key words and phrases that may aid in comprehension.

- ▶ Write questions sparked by the author's ideas.

The process of annotating, underlining, and highlighting helps students learn to engage actively with text. Eventually, they will be able to do this in their heads. If students are reading hard copies and they do not have their own books, make use of sticky notes.

Annotating will help students tremendously in becoming active readers since doing so forces students to be metacognitive—to think about their thinking. You can have a student annotate based on a specific skill. For instance, after a lesson on making an inference, you might require readers to underline and annotate parts of the text that led them to make an inference. Once you have taught all skills, students can choose how they wish to annotate. Giving students choice will make them feel empowered to think and interact authentically with the texts they are reading.

Ideally, you want to help students become completely engaged in an active reading experience so that they find that magical place where skilled readers go when they totally immerse themselves in the words of a book. Only when students gain the ability to do this will you be successful. One of the benefits of allowing students to read silently is that this silent reading time gives you an opportunity to meet with small groups of students with particular reading and writing needs and help them move toward higher achievement in critical areas.

Partner Reading

In addition to silent reading time, you should also give students opportunities to read aloud to one another. As they read out loud, you may want to work with students on reading with expression and even gesticulations. This "whole brain" reading approach not only keeps the reader focused, but it also keeps the listeners interested in the text. At times, students might listen to you read aloud with the group or listen to a recording of the book with headphones connected to a laptop or tablet. It is very important for students to have experiences not only reading silently but also hearing and following along with a good reader. The latter experience can significantly increase fluency. One of the teachers I observed several years ago asked students who were struggling with fluency to listen to an audio recording of a short text read by a fluent reader, and then to reread the short text out loud along with the recording. These struggling readers had greater test-score gains than struggling readers in any other teacher's class in the school.

Just as you expect students to focus and stay on task during silent reading, you should also have these high expectations when they read aloud with a partner or listen to a read-aloud or an audio recording. Again, you can use a simple rubric to reinforce the behaviors you want to see, such as the one below.

0	1	2	3
I did not stay focused or I interrupted my partner as we read.	I stayed focused some of the time but needed some redirection from my teacher.	I stayed focused most of the time, and when I was distracted, I was able to redirect myself.	I stayed intensely focused on reading the entire time.

Once students have spent several weeks developing positive reading habits, you will be able to begin meeting with small groups during in-class reading time. If you want your students to grow in literacy, then you absolutely cannot do anything but meet with small strategy practice groups during this time. As I pointed out in Chapter Four, research clearly shows that teachers who meet with individuals and small groups make the most significant impact on student achievement.

Chapter Six Summary

➤ Research shows that having eyes on text increases reading achievement levels.

➤ Training students to practice positive behaviors during this reading time is essential to student success.

➤ Providing students with daily opportunities for a variety of in-class reading experiences is essential. Students can read independently, with a partner, or follow along as the teacher reads or as they listen to an audio recording.

➤ Accountability will ensure that students are actually reading during silent and out-loud reading opportunities.

Strategies for Engaging and Motivating Readers

Challenging Students to Set Their Own Goals

We can learn a lot from the creators of video games. Children love video games because they constantly present challenges. They continuously measure the progress toward, and completion of, goals.

In my school in Chicago, the three teachers whose students performed at the highest levels all encouraged continual goal-setting from their students. These students learned to analyze their standardized test scores. They teased out the areas that needed the most focus, and then set specific goals on ways they would try to improve in these areas. Their students also set goals based on "soft" data such as behavior and formative assessments. The teachers frequently checked in on the students and monitored their progress toward the goals.

You will soon learn how you can utilize the online component of your blended classroom to communicate with students about their goals.

Using Standardized Test Data

We are a data-driven culture. Administrators and teachers continually analyze data to drive decisions about instruction. We spend our planning days combing through data. We write reports about it and set goals related to it. However, in my observations, few teachers share this data-driven, decision-making process with their students. The teachers who do have positive results.

When we think of data, often the first thing to come into our minds is high-stakes testing data. It is no wonder. Teachers are held accountable for showing gains on these assessments, so this data is naturally in the forefront of our minds during decision making. A principal might study this data to determine how well the school as a whole has performed, and a teacher might study this data to determine how well the classroom as a whole has performed. If we really intend to leave no child behind, we should study the data on an individual student basis, and we should let students be a part of the process of utilizing the information gleaned from the assessment to set goals for their improvement.

As I mentioned earlier, I have worked with teachers who share this data with their students. They meet with them individually and show them how to interpret the data. Then, the students can set informed short-term and long-term goals.

> ## A Student's Perspective
>
> " Setting goals for myself helped me improve my behavior and my reading. "
> —*Jorge, intermediate student*

On the Measures of Academic Progress (MAP) test, for instance, students can see their national percentile ranking in reading. They can also see specific reading strands so they know in which areas they need to work the hardest. Several years ago, I worked with a school system that administered the MAP for third through eighth graders in the fall, winter, and spring. After the fall scores, the teachers met with individual students and their parents to set goals based on the scores. Each student first set a goal for increasing their national percentile. Then, they created a plan for meeting that goal. The teachers for whom this goal-setting process produced positive results were the teachers who continually revisited these goals with their students and closely monitored progress toward the goals.

You could use a simple form like this for goal-setting based on a standardized test:

Name: Ima Goalsetter

Grade: 6

READING DATA:

Baseline (September)	Mid-year (January)	Target (May)
212	215	218

GOALS:

▶ To increase my score by six points so that I increase my percentile.

▶ To increase my vocabulary score, which was my lowest strand.

STRATEGIES FOR IMPROVEMENT:

▶ I will read every day in school and for thirty minutes at home.

▶ I will stay focused on reading during silent reading time, and I will reflect and write about reading during discussion board time.

▶ I will practice strategies for word analysis each day while I read.

Using Daily Data

In addition to setting long-term goals, the Chicago teachers who had the most gains in student achievement also set weekly or daily goals with their students.

When I taught reading, I required students to keep a weekly learning log. On Monday, as students entered class, they wrote the instructional objectives for the week and the strategies they would use to master the objectives on a goal-setting page. They also wrote behavior goals that would help them be more successful in meeting their academic goals. Finally, they wrote evidence to show how close they were to meeting their learning targets. This evidence could come in the form of self-assessment and/or teacher assessment. Examples of evidence include:

▶ Rubrics

▶ Quizzes

▶ Comments from the teacher during strategy practice group meetings

▶ Comments from the teacher and other students on the discussion board

If you have a class set of tablets or laptops, students can keep this log in a document on their devices. Then, at the end of the week, they can submit it to you electronically for accountability. Here is what a weekly data log might look like:

OBJECTIVE	STRATEGY	EVIDENCE OF MEETING TARGET
To make inferences supported by textual evidence	I will practice making inferences supported by textual evidence as I read the excerpt from the *Newsweek* article for my strategy practice group and as I read my book club book, *Bud, Not Buddy*. I will write about my process of making inferences on the discussion board. I will discuss inferences I have made in *Bud, Not Buddy* in my face-to-face meeting with my book club group.	Mrs. Pasisis said my inference was adequately supported by text evidence when I met with her in my strategy practice group. I received 8 out of 10 on my end of the week quiz. I received 3 out of 3 on the questions specific to inferences.
To work on staying focused during silent reading	I will choose a reading spot away from Travis, who always makes me laugh and distracts me. I will tune out anything going on around me and try to enter the reading zone.	I earned mostly 3s on my daily silent reading rubrics. On Wednesday and Thursday, I earned 2s because I was distracted for a short time due to being tired and not reading the whole time.
To submit substantive posts on the discussion board	Even though Mrs. Pasisis said to develop my own style for strategy reflections, I will temporarily go back to using the writing skeletons as a guide for making my posts more substantive.	In comparing this week's posts with last week's, I can see that my posts have more details and evidence to back up my ideas.
To follow the norms of my discussion group	I will remember to use my discussion chips when I want to contribute, and I will wait until it is my turn so that everyone has a chance to talk.	I spoke out of turn only once during my book club meeting.
To keep up with my reading at home	I will read thirty minutes each night in *Bud, Not Buddy* so that I can participate in the face-to-face discussions.	I am completely caught up on my book club reading goals.

Goals should be both instruction-focused and behavior-focused. As you will see after reading the next chapter, the two are inextricably intertwined.

Movement and Its Effect on Readers

A reading classroom involves a lot of sitting. That is just the reality of the type of work students do in a reading classroom. Students sit while they read, they sit while they write about reading, and they sit while they discuss.

In some schools, students sit not only in reading classes, but all day long. Grant Wiggins (2014) writes about a former teacher who followed two students for two days. She was exhausted at the end of each day because of the total lack of movement. As some administrators have become increasingly panicky about meeting school-wide expectations on state testing, they have cut physical education programs to give more minutes to classes that align to high-stakes tests. Reading, of course, is one of those classes.

Go online for a video demonstrating movement in the classroom. See page 154 for details.

I am certainly an advocate of giving as many minutes of instruction as possible to reading, but I would never add reading minutes at the expense of physical education minutes. Ironically, evidence that body movement affects brain performance is growing as fast as the childhood obesity epidemic that is caused in large part by the sedentary lifestyle of too many modern children.

A *New York Times* article reported the findings of an Irish study that showed the effects of exercise on the brain. Researchers studied changes in the brains of male college students after exercise. Before physical activity, the participants looked at a series of pictures and names. After a pause, they took a memory test. Next, half of the participants spent thirty minutes riding a stationary bicycle while the other half rested. All participants took the memory test again. The researchers found that the bike riders' scores increased while the scores of the sedentary participants remained the same (Reynolds, 2011).

In another study, female participants listened to two paragraphs read out loud and, after 35 minutes, they were asked to retell the content of what they heard. Participants who had ridden a stationary bicycle prior to listening to the paragraphs outperformed participants who did not exercise before the listening experience (Labban & Etnier, 2011). The findings in these studies indicate that exercise affects memory and recall, two elements that are of great importance in reading.

Dr. John Ratey (2008), a psychiatry professor at Harvard Medical School, gives a biological reason for this. He has researched the effects of exercise on a protein called BDNF, an acronym for brain-derived neurotrophic factor. In the mice he studied, exercise elevated levels of BDNF. Dr. Ratey calls BDNF "Miracle-Gro for the Brain" because the protein "nourishes neurons (brain cells) like fertilizer" (p. 19).

In the Irish study (Reynolds, 2011), researchers explained why the bike riding participants outperformed the sedentary participants by analyzing blood samples. They found that the bike riders' BDNF levels increased while the sedentary participants' levels remained stable. This provides a chemical explanation for the increase in the memory test scores.

Naperville Central High School in Naperville, Illinois, has focused on using body movements to impact students' minds in positive ways. By scheduling P. E. right before a student's most challenging class, the student can use exercise and its chemical effects to prime his or her brain for learning the challenging content. The effects have been huge. Students who participated in Naperville's Learning Readiness Physical Education Program increased reading achievement by, on average, half a year over those who did not (Iskander, 2011). At this high school, movement is not confined to P. E. classes. School leaders have asked all teachers to include movement and brain breaks in their classes. Some classrooms are even equipped with exercise bikes and balls.

How can you use this research to enhance your flipped and blended classroom? Read on for ideas!

Incorporating Movement Into Your Flipped Reading Block

As you have learned, movement is naturally a part of the flipped reading block. Because students are getting out of their chairs to work with partners, moving desks around to read or discuss with small groups, and moving to different parts of the room for different activities, movement is an inherent part of the program.

I suggest, though, that you take movement a step further. Considering the research, do what you can to make sure that your students have opportunities for a quality physical education class. Some schools have eliminated daily P. E., and if yours is one of those, fight for your students and urge school leaders to bring daily P. E. back. Also, if you have struggling readers, find ways for them to have an extended period of physical activity prior to reading class. At the elementary school level, this could mean scheduling your reading block shortly after P. E. or recess. The former teacher who shadowed non-moving students for two days said that, if she could go back in time and teach again, she would incorporate a stretch in the middle of her class, put a nerf basketball hoop in her classroom, and design a "move around" activity for each class period (Wiggins, 2014). At the middle school or high school level, you might work with administrators and counselors to schedule P. E. before reading and English classes for those students who are reading below grade level.

In addition to giving students a longer period of aerobic activity through physical education or recess activities, you can incorporate brain breaks into your classroom. In between activities, ask students to rise from their seats and move in simple ways. In a 2013 Eric Jensen training workshop I attended, he asked each group to assign one person to be a "stretch leader" and one person to be an "energizer." Throughout the four days of his presentation, he would stop periodically and ask the energizer of each group to lead the group in a body movement activity while he played upbeat music. Jensen modeled what should be happening in classrooms.

Your students could assign brain-break leaders in strategy practice groups and book clubs by appointing one person to the job. This person will lead the group in movement breaks at various times during the class.

In between activities, or whenever you feel the students need a brain break, play music while the groups move for a few minutes. When the music stops, direct students back to their working locations.

At the beginning of the year, you may want to lead the entire class in some activities. Tai Chi and yoga are great options because the movement and poses do not require running around (which can be difficult in small classroom spaces), but still give students aerobic exercise that uses large muscles. "Crouching Tiger" is a series of Tai Chi movements that my students have enjoyed. Yoga warrior poses are also popular among students. Traditional jumping jacks, one-foot hopping, and lunges are other options. Let your brain-break leaders decide which exercises to do.

Sometimes, a simple walk around the room can work wonders. You might start some music and then ask students to touch a window, a wall, a door, and the backs of five chairs before returning to their seats. This is a Jensen strategy that works! Just ninety

> ## A Student's Perspective
>
> " P.E. and recess are my favorite classes because we get to move and have fun.
> —*Jacob, intermediate student* "

Some Resources for Incorporating Movement

- ▸ *Brain Breaks for the Classroom* by Michelle Gay
- ▸ *Classroom Fitness Breaks to Help Kids Focus* by Sarah Longhi

The Flipped Reading Block © 2015 by Gina Pasisis, Scholastic Teaching Resources

seconds of walking may be enough to increase oxygen to the brain so that students can focus on the next task.

If your budget permits it, invest in some equipment that will promote movement. For students who have difficulty staying attentive during reading, you might buy stability balls. Some teachers have found that the muscles needed to remain stable on the balls actually help fidgety students concentrate. Also, you might consider a portable, folding cycle. Students can sit in a chair and read or post on the discussion board while pedaling. Koosh balls are an inexpensive investment that could give you a great bang for your buck. Throwing these balls around during discussion, students can multi-task and oxygenate the brain through movement *and* talking.

Chapter Seven Summary

- ▶ Learn from the creators of video games and engage students in setting goals for themselves and tracking their progress.

- ▶ Teach students to analyze their own standardized assessment data to set their own goals for improvement.

- ▶ Require that students set weekly goals related to both instructional objectives and behavior.

- ▶ Findings of recent studies show that exercise affects memory and recall, two elements of great importance in reading.

- ▶ Ensuring that students have chances for extended periods of exercise, such as experiences offered in a quality physical education program, could increase reading achievement for your students.

- ▶ In addition to physical education classes, you can increase focus and oxygen to the brain by giving students brain breaks during class.

Managing Blended Reading Groups

Classroom Management Matters!

I don't really think that I ever, as a teacher, fully understood the connection between classroom management and reading achievement. In the U.S. Department of Education Institute of Education Sciences 2010 report, the item that showed the highest correlation between teacher practice and reading achievement was the "teachers' management and responsiveness" (James-Burdumy et. al., 2010, p. xxii). Without a well-managed classroom, the most perfectly designed literacy program would fail.

At this point, you have read about a classroom that combines online activities, face-to-face activities, teacher-student collaboration, student-student collaboration, independent reading and writing activities, and movement. I have observed classrooms in which this design promotes strong classroom management. However, my experience has shown that the teachers who make this work are the ones who create an environment conducive to a blend of active learning strategies. This environment cannot be created with the wave of a magic wand. It takes planning.

Setting Up a Modern Reading Classroom and Creating Space for Optimal Learning

I have watched teachers spend weeks in the summer decorating their classrooms. I have never known a teacher who did not wish for a classroom that invites students to learn. In the well-managed classrooms I have visited, teachers have carefully selected lighting, made the best use of wall space, and arranged furniture to create an atmosphere that allows students to learn.

> Go online to see a video tour of classrooms that incorporate a flipped reading block. See page 154 for details.

The Best Lighting for Learning

One simple way to create a soothing, peaceful space for reading and thinking is to choose soft lighting for the classroom. Most schools utilize fluorescent lighting because it is cheap, but this lighting can stimulate the brain in ways that are not conducive to learning. It can overstimulate students prone to hyperactivity and anxiety. If you have fluorescent lighting, investigate covers for the lights. I have even heard of teachers obtaining grants for these covers in order to improve behavior of their students. Use natural lighting when you can. If you have a wall of windows, open the shades. Perhaps you could only turn on half of the fluorescent lights in the classroom. You might also consider investing in some inexpensive lamps to create ambient light.

Eliminating harsh lighting can have positive results. Rita Dunn and Shirley Griggs found that soft lighting can even result in higher test scores (2004). As you choose your lighting, make sure that each student has sufficient light at his or her desk. Sit at each desk and see for yourself that the lighting will not cause eye strain. Students in your class need to feel comfortable as they spend time with eyes on text. You must find "Goldilocks lighting" that is not too bright or too dim, but just right. You will know when you find the perfect balance.

A Student's Perspective

" Open the blinds and let natural light in.
—Emma, middle-school student

Wall Space Considerations

How you cover wall space is another important consideration. Certainly, you do not want empty walls, but you also do not want to create a cluttered environment. Clutter can create a sense of uneasiness, while ordered space can create inner calm. In every cluttered classroom I have entered, I have noticed students who seem to match the environment. In classrooms that are more orderly, students are calmer and more focused.

Choose carefully what you put on your walls. Students notice everything you hang. In my classroom, I had a quote wall. For instance, I posted the Eleanor Roosevelt quote, "No one can make you feel inferior without your consent." All year long, students saw this quotation every day. My hope is that they will remember it when they encounter those inevitable situations in which others try to make them feel inferior.

Don't forget to leave space to celebrate your learners. Show them that you value their thoughts and contributions by hanging their work. On my quote wall, I hung several famous quotes that I wanted students to remember, but most of the space was reserved for quotes by my students. On a table in the classroom, I kept a basket containing strips and markers. If a student heard another student say something "quote-wall worthy," the student wrote the quote on the strip and added it to the quote wall. Students loved this wall. It was like Twitter without potentially dangerous, uncensored language. During passing time, there were always students hanging around the wall reading what their colleagues had said. A student quote wall not only celebrates learners, but it also encourages critical thinking.

You will also want to hang important messages about the learning. Here are some posters every reading classroom should contain all year long:

- ▶ the reading behaviors necessary for students to experience success during silent reading time

- ▶ the writing behaviors necessary during online learning on the discussion board

- ▶ the norms for collaborative, face-to-face learning

As a teacher, I always put anchor charts for new learning on the front walls and then moved those charts to the side walls when students had mastered the concepts and only needed the posters for reference. You can also use the walls to help students visualize class goals. As your students increase their ability to let words flow as they write, you may put up a chart of the number of minutes all students in the class write without stopping. You can show how the time increases from day to day as you develop positive writing behaviors with your students.

Designing the Space for Movement

In a classroom that incorporates student movement, as I hope your classroom will, you need to carefully consider creating a space that is conducive to this active learning. In order to have learners who move smoothly from one seating arrangement to another, you must plan procedures and strategies that will keep movement orderly. Teachers generally like the idea of a classroom where active learning is taking place. What stops many teachers from adopting this modern approach to teaching is the fear of losing control. The anxiety resulting from the vision of a classroom gone mad, with students hanging from the ceiling tiles, inspires them to stick to the old school methods that ensure order. The problem is that teachers married to old school ways are finding that these methods no longer work for maintaining order. Some modern learners resist them and become agitated by teachers who don't meet their needs. I watched this occur in a classroom in which the teacher, afraid of losing control, never let students talk or move. Her plan backfired. Students developed a hatred of her, they rebelled, and she lost control anyway. No matter how many times she said, "Please stop talking" and "please stay seated," she could not motivate them to cooperate.

Here is the good news: It is possible to create a classroom that allows movement and collaboration without sacrificing order. The key to that environment lies in a proactive teacher, who designs the classroom space so that movement will be easy and creates procedures that promote order.

> ## A Student's Perspective
>
> **"** A teacher should be nice, but strict enough to keep order in the classroom. **"**
> —*Alex, middle-school student*

> ## A Student's Perspective
>
> **"** Do group activities and move students around so that they don't get bored. **"**
> —*Prakar, middle-school student*

Furniture arrangement is very important in the modern classroom. Many arrangements work, but the arrangement should allow students to move easily. A kidney shaped table is a huge advantage for a classroom. The teacher can meet with strategy practice groups at this table while the other students read silently and/or participate in online discussions.

As far as student desk arrangement, one of my favorites is this one:

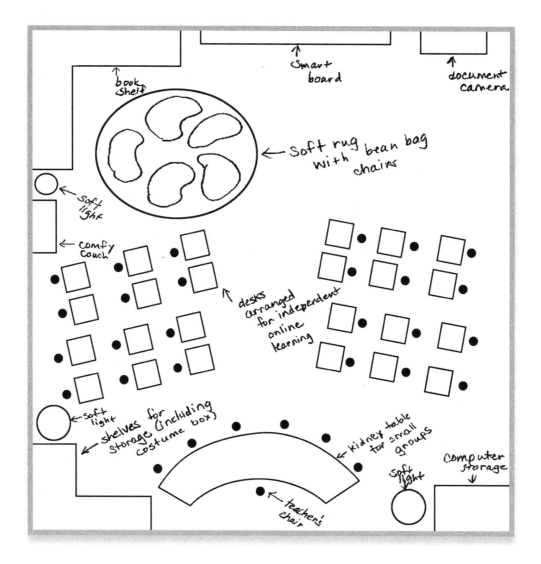

In this arrangement, students can learn independently. This would be a good arrangement when students are working on the discussion board. From this arrangement, students can also easily turn to a partner and work in pairs, or easily move into small groups.

In the next drawing, you can see how the classroom is easily transformed from an independent learning formation to a collaborative learning formation with a simple movement of student desks.

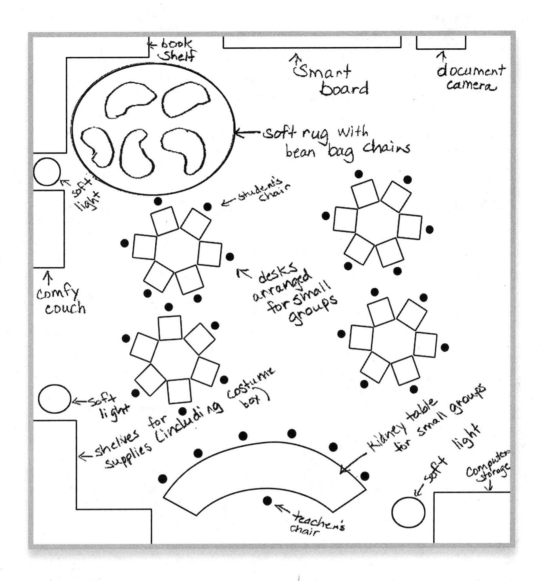

When students move from one arrangement to another, chaos can easily ensue if you have not prepared procedures and trained students to follow them. The sheer noise of the desk movement can be enough to trigger off-task behavior. A remedy for this noise problem is the simple tennis ball. By making an x-shaped cut in a tennis ball, the ball will fit perfectly on a leg of the desk. I approached a tennis pro at a local tennis club and asked for donations of used tennis balls. People are usually happy to help their community by making a donation to a classroom, especially in a case like this because the donation does not cost a penny! If your school can afford new furniture, ask for the rolling desks designed for easy moving.

Plan Procedures

Positive classroom management involves considering every detail, even the smallest one. This involves a procedures plan that includes explicit expectations and opportunities for students to practice procedures until they do exactly what the teacher wants them to do. In this section, you will read about some of the procedures every teacher should consider.

Procedures for Moving Into a Variety of Formations

You must teach students how to move into a variety of formations quickly. In a flipped classroom approach, students may start class in an independent learning formation. After the independent learning activity, they may move to work with partners. Then, they might move into their strategy practice group formation or their book club formation. When students move into the various formations, the teacher must show each student exactly where his or her desk must move. I use decorations on the ceiling so that each student has a "landmark." It takes quite a bit of time before school even begins to practice moving desks into different formations and to record the "landmarks" for each student in each different formation, but it will be well worth it when students learn to move quickly to the exact place they need to be to begin a collaborative activity.

During the first three weeks of school, it is imperative to have students practice the procedures of moving into different formations. For each formation, I give students a specific number of seconds to move. I require that there is no talking at all during that movement so that I do not risk losing students to off-task discussions. I say, for instance, "You have fifteen silent seconds to move into book clubs. Go." I begin counting backward from fifteen with my fingers. Students move their desks toward their landmarks, and while they are doing it, they look to me to see how they are doing on time. When students make it to their formation in time, I praise them and remind them that their cooperation will ensure that they have opportunities for active learning. They are so appreciative of teachers who give them opportunities to work with other students and collaborate that they are willing to cooperate.

A Student's Perspective

> If the teacher has order, we don't waste time.
>
> —Stephanie, middle-school student

Once they have reached their new spots in the formation, you should give explicit instructions on the activity that will follow. Students must know exactly when they are allowed to talk, and procedures must be in place to ensure that students maintain order and stay on task while they are working in small groups. Review Chapter Three to reread scripts that demonstrate these explicit instructions.

The Flipped Reading Block © 2015 by Gina Pasisis, Scholastic Teaching Resources

If students store their laptops or tablets at school, you should create a storage space for them and set up a procedure for checking them out. At the beginning of the year, you may wish to assign each student a number that corresponds to the student's computer. That way, you will not waste time by asking students to stand in line for long periods of time while students write their names to check out computers. Again, you must establish those habits early. This is another time when ceiling "landmarks" can be helpful. On one side of the classroom, you might put the pictures of famous novelists on the ceiling. On the other side of the classroom, you might cover the ceiling with poets. Then, when it is time to check out computers, say to your class, "Each student on the novelist's side of the classroom should line up quietly and take his or her computer." Meanwhile, give students on the poet's side of the classroom a task to occupy them during this transition. Then, say, "Now, each student on the poet's side of the classroom should line up quietly and take his or her computer." Again, address the students on the novelist's side, and give them a task so that no instructional time is lost with off-task behavior.

A Plan for the Crucial First Minutes of Class

A plan for the beginning of each class period is of huge importance, as the first few minutes of class set the tone for the rest of the period. If students are off-task, wandering around and socializing, it will be difficult to grab their attention for the rest of the period. I require that my students be not only in the room but also at their desks when the bell rings. Projected on my screen is an agenda and what has traditionally been called a "bell ringer," an activity that students must get right to work on as soon as the bell rings. Even though I always plan time for students to talk with one another at some point during the period, I prefer to begin class quietly, giving students an opportunity to become mentally prepared for the day's learning.

Even in the modern classroom, teachers are expected to attend to administrative tasks such as taking attendance, collecting field trip forms, lunch count, etc. This is a time when students often get off-task and waste precious instructional time. Typically, this occurs at the beginning of the period, the time that sets the tone for the rest of the period. Therefore, it is essential to have a procedure in place for this crucial three to five minutes. Here are some suggestions:

- ▶ If you have a classroom set of netbooks, laptops, or tablets, you may wish to use this time for students to log in.

- ▶ Students could begin class by writing the objective and the strategy for achieving the objective in their learning logs.

- ▶ You could begin class with a "do now" activity, such as short reading passage and question that assesses a skill that was worked on the day before or that serves as an entrance ticket that shows an understanding of a video-recorded lesson that students were expected to watch for homework. This is the perfect opportunity to connect to the previous day's learning.

Bathroom Procedures

Consider having a plan for when students must go to the bathroom. As natural as this need is, I have known many teachers who struggle in deciding when to allow students to leave class and go to the bathroom. If students must ask the teacher before going to the bathroom, class is disrupted. Frequent trips cause a student to miss learning experiences, and some students will use the bathroom excuse to escape learning. Despite all this, I have never been a teacher who could say, "You may only go to the bathroom twice a semester." That just seems inhumane.

Tell students at the beginning of the year what the procedure is for going to the bathroom. I have observed classrooms that use sign language when students ask for permission to go to the bathroom. The student signs the word for bathroom, and then the teacher signs back with either "yes" or "later." This type of bathroom request causes no interruption. I always remind students that it is in their best interest to go to the bathroom during a passing period so that they will not miss valuable instruction, but I also understand that nature does not always call at precise times. In most cases, students are so grateful for the respect I show them that they do not abuse the privilege.

A Student's Perspective

" Let students go to the bathroom.
—*Phil, middle-school student* "

Also, I try to plan engaging, irresistible learning that students do not want to miss. However, in the few cases during which a student seems to go to the bathroom too often, I simply talk to the student. "You seem to be leaving class often to go to the bathroom. Is there a way I can help you to organize your time better so you can use the bathroom during passing period and not miss so many learning opportunities?" That is usually all it takes to prevent students from abusing the privilege. For one extreme case, I talked with the student and said, "I am very concerned about instructional minutes lost during your numerous trips to the bathroom. Can we plan some time during lunch or after school to make up these minutes? Your learning matters to me." This ended the behavior of missing class unnecessarily. Be sure that you are aware of each student's medical needs, and never make a student with a medical condition feel uncomfortable about leaving class whenever he or she needs to do so. Even though you have given students permission to go to the bathroom when they need to do so, you still need a procedure in place. I find it helpful to keep one girl's and one boy's hall pass hanging by the front door. Beside the passes,

I place a sign out sheet. Students must sign out and take a pass in order to go to the bathroom, and I then have a record that helps me decide if I need to have a talk with any individual student.

Collecting Papers

Another important procedure you must have in place on the first day of school is your system for collecting papers. With more and more schools providing netbooks, tablets, or individual computers for students, we are moving toward a paperless system. Some teachers, though, still prefer hard copies for grading some assignments. And some teachers, who are accustomed to our old system of hard copies, may have concerns that it will take more time to grade papers electronically. I urge you to give e-grading a chance. Even a digital immigrant like me has embraced this new technology. It has many benefits. First, no student can ever approach a teacher and say, "I turned in my paper yesterday." With electronic submission, the teacher knows the exact date and time. The student can't say, "My dog ate my homework." While dogs do have an attraction to paper, no dog, to my knowledge, has ever eaten a computer. Finally, it is very convenient to comment on writing electronically. In Microsoft Word, for example, a teacher could use the "Track Changes" feature. Using a tablet, the teacher could use a stylus to write comments in the margins. The best news is that this process is paperless. Save trees! No more back problems caused by lugging home notebooks and papers! Less germ exposure! Easier record keeping! The benefits really seem endless.

Some schools do not have the money for computers for every student, though, and there are still tasks for which a paper and pencil system is more appropriate. Therefore, you should have a system for collecting and returning hard copy assignments. I like to collect papers at the beginning of the period while students work on the bell ringer task. For daily assignments that do not carry as much weight, I divide the class into four areas and ask a student to be responsible for collecting the papers in each area.

For major projects and assignments, I collect the papers myself. That way, I know right away if any particular student does not have the assignment to submit, and I can coach and counsel that student to get it turned in right away. I also use this time at the beginning of the class to return papers. As I collect assignments, I do so based on the seating arrangement. That way, when I return papers, it is also quick. I have a set of "to be graded" bins and a set of "to be returned" bins. This system makes it easy for me to stay organized, and I NEVER lose a student paper. Believing that students deserve as much privacy in their academic records as patients do with their medical records, I never allow students to hand out the graded papers. Just as a patient would not want a doctor to pass a medical report around a community, students do not want a teacher to reveal academic performance to the classroom community. A grade should be a private matter between the student and the teacher.

Establishing a Positive Classroom Culture From Day One

Once you have determined your procedures, you are ready to begin creating plans for the crucial first few days of school. As you can tell, one of the keys to be a successful modern reading teacher is planning. With good strategies in place, you cannot fail!

> Go online to view a video demonstrating some strategies for creating a positive classroom climate. See page 154 for details.

The Power of a Smile

I don't think I fully realized the power of a teacher's smile until I received this note from a student. The words will be forever etched in my memory: "You have been my favorite teacher because you are the only teacher who ever smiled at me."

Well, I guess that makes perfect sense! All the other poor teachers have been the victims of the same advice I received as a first year teacher: don't smile until Christmas.

As humans, we are conditioned to observe subtle nuances in facial expressions. An expression of anger from a teacher can make students feel anxious, and this anxiety can actually paralyze learning. Even short-term anxiety can activate stress hormones and release them in the hippocampus, the brain's center for learning and memory (Nauert, 2008). As stress hormones fire in their brains, learners enter a state of fear that can make them unable to focus. On the other hand, a smile may make students feel reassured, cared about, and calm. Without the rapid firing of stress hormones, their brains function better. Students need to be in this relaxed state as they work on improving their reading skills. After all, some students face numerous obstacles when learning to read. They need as much support as you can give them to approach these obstacles with confidence rather than run away from them in fear.

Putting students in the right frame of mind for learning should happen on day one. Students are always nervous on the first day. In fact, many say that they have little memory of the details of the first day of school, and it is because of the brain's reaction to generalized anxiety. A teacher's warm smile may create a sense of calm that will impact learning on that critical first day and beyond. In the student survey I conducted, the most reported component of effective teaching was a teacher's smile! That was surprising but powerful data.

A Student's Perspective

> There is nothing worse than a teacher who comes in with a stern face, lectures for an hour, and then dismisses class with a stern face.
> —*Megan, middle-school student*

The Flipped Reading Block © 2015 by Gina Pasisis, Scholastic Teaching Resources

The brain learns quickly to associate emotions with different environments. If your students feel peaceful and are consequently able to learn on the first day, the same thing will happen on day two, day three, and throughout the remainder of the year.

Do not mistake a smile as a sign of weakness; it is instead a sign of strength. When a teacher stands by the door greeting students with a smile, the students infer that they are entering a classroom with a teacher who knows how to teach. As a result, they will not close their minds to that teacher's learning strategies. You don't want your reading class to be the class that students tune out. Train their brains from day one to flip the switch to "on" when they enter your classroom.

Knowing the positive effects of a smile, I smile every day, and I have the wrinkles to prove it! Even on days when I am tired or feeling a little low for whatever reason, I force myself to smile. Soon, I have students and other teachers smiling back at me and my spirit is lifted. When we hear that a smile is contagious, it really is!

In this chapter, I discuss multiple strategies to condition student brains for learning, but I believe a teacher's genuine smile is most important of all.

Hooking Students and Establishing a Positive Culture

On the first day, students are consciously and unconsciously making assessments of teachers and curriculum. The results of those assessments will affect student achievement for the rest of the year.

The human brain knows how to sort information into two categories: worthy of storage and unworthy of storage. Although we don't realize it is happening, our brains are constantly deciding which information to keep and which information to discard or reject. We naturally retain information that is personally relevant and discard information that is meaningless (Bernard, 2010). On the first day

> ## A Student's Perspective
>
> " I value a teacher who makes learning worthwhile. "
> —*Rachel, middle-school student*

of school, students' brains are making these decisions. Therefore, a teacher should show students the relevance of the class.

When I had my own reading class, for instance, I asked students to divide into groups and compile a list of uses for reading, writing, and speaking skills. After synthesizing the group lists, I posted a class list, which remained posted as a reminder all year. Here are a few of the items students listed:

- ▶ to be able to comprehend challenging text
- ▶ to enjoy reading
- ▶ to perform better on high-stakes tests
- ▶ to learn about all subjects through the development of a higher reading ability

▸ to expand my vocabulary so that I can communicate better

▸ to enhance my critical thinking skills so that I can develop my own personal code of ethics

In this activity, students themselves determined the reasons they should pay attention in my class, and that empowered them and made them want to learn. Understanding how a class can make significant changes in their lives triggers students' brains to create storage space for the content of the class.

Many teachers begin the first day of school with school rules. I don't believe this is effective. Some students just say to themselves, "I don't know if I care enough about this teacher or this class to want to obey the rules, so I'm not going to pay attention." Therefore, they take a brain holiday, and the teacher's lecture about rules falls on deaf ears. I always have chosen to establish a code of behavior only after the students have already found their own personal relevance in the course. When students decide a class is worthy of their attention, they will care enough to want to learn the expectations for their behavior.

I have observed numerous teachers who have created a democratic classroom. Fay and Funk (1995), in *Teaching With Love and Logic*, remind teachers to give students power on teachers' terms. Otherwise, students will take power on their own terms. How true this is! On day two in my reading classroom, I gave students the power to decide how our classroom would function as they worked collaboratively. Each group had the task of creating one law that would guide the behavior of all of us, including me, the teacher. I reminded them to create a law that would ensure an environment that promotes learning for all. By having students work in groups, the number or rules is limited to a reasonable number. I recall a teacher whose list of rules was so long that it began at the ceiling and ended at the floor! In that class, I felt doomed to failure from the start. If I could not possibly remember all the rules, I felt I was sure to break some.

After the groups created their one law, I appointed one student the task of leading the class to combine all of the group ideas into one law that represented the desires and needs of everyone. Every time I have gone through this exercise, students have arrived at the same overarching law: Respect everyone. Sometimes, the words are different, like, "Consider the needs of all people in the classroom" or "Treat everyone as you want to be treated," but the meaning is always the same. Students know how we, as humans, should behave in a civilized world.

> ## A Student's Perspective
>
> " I pay more attention when the teacher trusts me to make some decisions.
> —*Sydney, middle-school student* "

Once we decided on the wording of our law, we discussed what it meant. The students might say, "This means that we should listen when other people are talking"

The Flipped Reading Block © 2015 by Gina Pasisis, Scholastic Teaching Resources

or "We should respect ourselves by giving our best effort." Students then made a list of things an outsider might observe when coming into this classroom of law-abiding citizens. Students, whose minds were now opened and primed for learning, inscribed this law into their brains, and we hung the poster just in case the inscription became slightly faded at times.

I always told students that I would do my best to abide by the law as well. That meant I must respect them enough to challenge them intellectually and to invest time and effort into planning and facilitating meaningful activities. I would fairly assess their progress and provide them with opportunities to learn in differentiated ways. An effective teacher wants students to say to themselves, "Wow. This teacher really cares. I want to please her."

My observations of teachers have shown me this: When students feel learning is meaningful and relevant, and when they respect a teacher who cares enough to create engaging and powerful lessons, they rarely misbehave. Still, posting the law (and what obeying it means) serves as a reminder for the rest of the year.

After creating the classroom law, students must decide on problem-solving strategies to assist students who are having difficulty obeying it. Remind students that the activities are not meant to be punitive in nature. Instead, they are meant to assist students as they search for solutions to help them be the best citizens of the community that they can be.

Some ideas students may come up with include:

▶ Spend a lunch period brainstorming solutions with the teacher.

▶ Spend a lunch period brainstorming solutions with another student.

▶ Move my seat to a new spot where I won't have distractions from my friend.

▶ Write a behavior plan that includes strategies for behavior improvement.

▶ Call my parents to ask them to help problem-solve.

▶ Write an apology letter to the person injured by my actions.

▶ Complete a community-service project.

▶ Meet with the teacher after school for a problem-solving session.

▶ Meet with another student after school for a problem-solving session.

▶ Go to the counselor's or principal's office so he or she can provide solutions.

Usually, by the end of day two, I noticed that students already felt that they were an important part of the classroom community. As they worked in groups, getting to know others in the class as they brainstormed ideas, I circulated, making an effort to make individual contact and build relationships with each student. I know the importance of relationship-building; for if I succeed, the student will feel safe in my class and will want to work for me.

Some teachers, in the first few days, will ask students to introduce themselves to the class. I feel this activity is an exercise in futility. In the past, I have asked students if this helps them to get to know each other. They say it does not because they are so nervous about speaking before the entire group that they never listen to what the other students say. In a class of twenty to thirty students, asking each student to give a personal introduction also takes too much time. You have a short window of opportunity to make students feel empowered to learn and can't afford to spend time on an activity unrelated to that purpose. Besides, with the community-building activities I recommend, students get to know each other as they collaborate. In the first week of class, vary the group assignments each day. Before all group activities, ask students to introduce themselves to their small groups. By the end of the week, all students will have the opportunity to meet all others in the class without the stress of public speaking before a large group during those anxiety-filled first days. As a teacher, I am continually thinking of ways to create a comfortable environment because I understand fully the effects of calmness on the brain and learning.

In a classroom where a teacher is constantly working with small groups, it is important that the students learn how to function without constant intervention. You must build capacity in students to be contributing members of the classroom. This can be accomplished through the creation of a high-functioning community, complete with jobs for each member. To design the community, I asked students to work in groups again, and this time I asked them to create a list of jobs necessary to keep our learning community running smoothly. In the real world, job descriptions change constantly. In this microcosm of the bigger world, job descriptions evolve during the year, as well.

Here are some possibilities of jobs students will come up with:

- ▶ Collectors (for the times when hard copies are produced)
- ▶ Editors (for any classroom website or newsletter)
- ▶ Mediators (to assist in resolving conflict among community members)
- ▶ Encouragers (to praise positive behaviors)
- ▶ Bankers (if you have a classroom money system)
- ▶ Buyers (to find enticing classroom rewards to order)
- ▶ Summarizers (to summarize key information)
- ▶ Brain-break leaders (to lead movement in between activities)
- ▶ Zoologists (if you have classroom pets)
- ▶ Gardeners (if you have classroom plants)
- ▶ Marine biologists (if you have fish)
- ▶ Librarians (to check out books from the classroom library)
- ▶ Computer technicians (to problem-solve computer malfunctions)
- ▶ Attendance clerks (keep in mind that attendance documents are legal, so always double check attendance yourself)

- ▶ Technology leaders (to set up the interactive whiteboard, document camera, or any other technology)
- ▶ Discussion leaders (this job rotates)

Once students have decided on the jobs, you can ask groups to create job descriptions for the jobs they feel are most important. Thinking about the skills and behaviors required for each of the jobs, they might also create applications for the jobs. Since job assignments will change periodically, everyone will have a chance, at some point in the year, to enjoy his or her first choice.

To encourage a strong sense of community, you might ask students to vote on a classroom name. They may decide to call their class Smith Village or Smithtown if they are Mr. Smith's community of learners. After a few nominations, you can let the classroom vote, even if the process is as informal as "put your head on your desk and hold up your hand when you hear the name for which you wish to vote."

Although it will require more time for students to be involved in the process of setting up the classroom community, it is essential that they do so. As you begin reading instruction, students will work independently, with various partners, and as a part of strategy practice groups and book clubs. You, as the teacher, need to be free to work with small groups and individuals, so you must put into place a community of independent learners who all contribute to the functioning of the classroom. As adults, these students will be a part of many communities. In addition to a work community, a community in which they live, and possibly a worship community, they will be a part of the global community. It is valuable, therefore, for you to help students understand the importance of being an active, contributing member of a community of learners in preparation for their future roles within communities in the adult world.

Don't Let Intervention Paralysis Destroy Your Classroom Culture

Let's say your few days of school have passed, and you are feeling good about your reading classroom. You have begun to establish a culture of collaboration, one that will translate easily into the modern real world. Students have created the classroom law and know the significance of positive learning behaviors. What do you do now to show students that you will hold them accountable if they fail to meet the expectations established by the community of learners? This is the point in time at which some teachers make a wrong turn down a difficult path, one that can lead to distress. Once on this path, it is possible to return to the good path, but the journey will be an uphill climb that will exhaust you and your students. How can teachers avoid those difficult roads? The answer is simple: You must intervene when students do not meet the expectations the classroom community has created. Although the answer is simple, putting the answer into practice is very hard.

Teachers are caring and nurturing by nature. For that reason, we often hesitate to punish a student whose behavior does not meet our expectations. The thought of causing pain for a student causes us pain. I can remember times during my first year of teaching when I actually experienced a physical reaction, the feeling of a stab to the heart, when I asked students to stay after school for detention. When I saw how providing some type of redirection helped my students improve behavior, though, that stab-in-the-heart feeling ceased.

When we fail to redirect students whose behaviors inhibit learning, we are actually harming them. In fact, when a student's behavior prevents learning, a reasonable, individualized intervention, delivered with compassion and a true spirit of helpfulness, is actually the most caring teacher behavior.

A Student's Perspective

" Rather than punishing students for getting in trouble in class, it is better to help them understand what they can improve on. "
—*Paul, middle-school student*

In my early years of teaching, I developed the list of classroom rules myself and I had a list of punishments in a particular order. It was all black and white, but as distinguished educator Rick Wormeli (2006) has taught us, "Fair isn't always equal." We have to evaluate each student behavior individually. A concrete list of punishments has never delivered positive long-term results. After all, what fits one "offense" does not necessarily fit another, and a strategy that works for one student may not work for another.

To accommodate all students' needs, we need to make the plan for consequences flexible. Now, even as I model instruction in other teacher's classrooms, I let students know that the plan for consequences will be individualized to meet each specific student's needs. I tell them that even though the consequence may feel like a punishment, this is not my intention. Instead, I will be working with them and their parents to find solutions that will increase opportunities for learning. A traditional detention, at which a student must simply sit quietly during coveted lunch or after-school time, is clearly just a punishment. However, a consequence that causes the student to reflect on the behavior and create an action plan for behavior improvement is not a punishment. I learned about the difference between a punishment and a consequence by reading *Teaching With Love and Logic* (Fay & Funk, 1995), a book that completely changed the way I managed my classroom. From this wisely written book, I learned to support a student in developing his or her own solutions to obstacles that impede learning. Fay and Funk caution us, as teachers, against making all the

The Flipped Reading Block © 2015 by Gina Pasisis, Scholastic Teaching Resources

decisions and doing all the problem-solving for our students. After all, it is through engaging in the problem-solving process that people change their behaviors. In the real world, we must find solutions to all sorts of complex problems. We may need to learn to deal with difficult bosses and co-workers. We may have broken relationships with spouses or friends. We must fix what is broken within ourselves, as well. Why not start helping students do that now?

On the first or second day of school, as soon as the classroom expectations have been established, you should begin holding students accountable for meeting them. Let's say a student has a problem with talking at inappropriate times. This is, believe it or not, the classroom management problem that causes the most damage to a classroom. Although teachers sometimes face much bigger problems, such as violence and drugs, the problem they most *often* face is inappropriate talking that makes it impossible for them to teach. If, for instance, a student blurts out responses in discussion groups without waiting for his turn, you might pull the student aside and whisper, "Please meet with me at lunch." "For what?" the student asks. "To work together and create a solution." Leave it at that! At lunch, sit down with the student and say, "I am worried that you are not respecting yourself or your peers. Not only are you inhibiting your learning by talking at inappropriate times, but you are also failing to show respect to your colleagues. I would like for you to reflect on your behavior and search for interventions that will help you make better decisions. I believe in you and want you to succeed." Again, this is not a detention. The word "detention" means the state of being detained. It signals punishment and nothing more. Having a student come in during lunch to talk with the teacher rather than holding the student for detention sends a message that this meeting really is not intended to be a punishment. A meeting during which you talk with the student is an opportunity to find resolutions that will prevent the behavior from happening again. In this instance, you have kindly and firmly intervened to redirect.

My students quickly understood this distinction. I always emphasized that the purpose was to help improve behavior because I cared about the student's learning and well-being. Giving up my time during lunch demonstrated that I would make personal sacrifices to make sure that all students had the opportunity to reach their full potential. It is less likely that students will become angry and build walls against you when they can see that your actions come from a sense of caring.

If you are a teacher who uses lunch with the teacher as a reward, do not worry that students will try to get into trouble just to have these lunch meetings with you. They won't. Reward lunches are fun. Mine involved several students who played games or watched a movie while they ate. Intervention lunches are not fun. It is hard work to reflect on poor choices and create a plan for improvement.

I like to hold intervention meetings during lunch when possible, but you can hold these meetings before school, after school, or anytime that is convenient for you. If you start these meetings at the beginning of the year while you can nip problems in the bud, you will not need to have many of them. The time invested will be well worth the returns when you have a happy, wholesome learning environment with engaged, well-behaved learners. You may miss a few lunches or free periods early in the year, but you will save yourself long days and sleepless nights later on by being proactive from the start.

If your first meeting with a student does not cure behavior, consider asking the student to create his or her own more detailed behavior improvement plan. Below you will find a sample form that you could use to assist your students in making these decisions. Remind students that they developed a possible list of solutions for behavior problems during the first week of school. Students can refer to that list when they complete this form, or they can come up with their own ideas.

When using this form:

1. Have a clipboard containing the behavior improvement plans handy while you are teaching.

2. If a student does not meet your expectations, meet briefly with the student outside of class to let the student know which behavior is causing a problem.

3. If the student does not meet your expectations a second time, plan a time to meet again with the student. Then, during the meeting, work together to fill out the form. Remind the student that he or she is not being punished, but is instead being given time to reflect quietly on a plan of action to improve behavior so that he or she can learn. The student must think about what interventions he or she will prescribe. The act of writing them down will burn them into the mind. The choice of interventions (however limited that choice is) will empower the student. Your learners will know that they can control whether or not these interventions happen.

4. At the end of the meeting, make sure both you and the student sign the form, then keep it handy while you are teaching.

5. If the student fails to meet the classroom community expectations again, turn to the form (it is good to keep them in alphabetical order), initial the intervention, and whisper to the student, "Please move to another seat during online discussion board time." If the student argues, say, "I will not argue with you now, as I do not wish to embarrass you in front of your colleagues. You may certainly write me a written argument after you complete the intervention that you planned, or we can meet right after school today to talk about this if you would like." Smile genuinely, and continue teaching. The line between the consequence and the class instruction is seamless. Little time is lost.

Natural consequences exist in the real world. Consequence help us to reconsider behavior. Your classroom is a miniature version of the bigger world, so you can prepare students by intervening when a student needs redirection.

The Flipped Reading Block © 2015 by Gina Pasisis, Scholastic Teaching Resources

Name _____

Behavior Improvement Plan

Describe the behavior/behaviors hindering your ability to learn.

(to be completed at a quiet time so you can reflect)

POSSIBLE SOLUTION #1 _____

Why will this help you?

POSSIBLE SOLUTION #2 _____

Why will this help you?

POSSIBLE SOLUTION #3 _____

Why will this help you?

POSSIBLE SOLUTION #4 _____

Why will this help you?

POSSIBLE SOLUTION #5 _____

Why will this help you?

Student signature _____

Teacher signature _____

A Strong Reinforcement System

In addition to holding students accountable for meeting expectations and providing interventions when they do not, you should also offer a system of incentives and positive reinforcement. In the real world, insurance companies give discounts to drivers who don't have traffic violations. In our classroom, we should reward students who exhibit behaviors that contribute to a positive classroom community.

You might consider incentives for exhibiting positive behaviors. For instance, at the end of each week, a student who has consistently participated actively with a positive attitude may earn fifteen minutes of time to spend on a creative endeavor of his or her choice. If all students in the class have earned this reward, you can allow them to watch ten or fifteen minutes of a movie, or enjoy fifteen minutes of free time outside. Some teachers may worry that fifteen minutes is a long time to take away from valuable instruction. However, looking at the big picture, you can see that good behavior for a week will actually save valuable instruction time. Really, fifteen minutes a week only works out to be three minutes a day. Think about that. How many minutes are lost when you must redirect and redirect and redirect?

You should also offer many words of praise to students who demonstrate appropriate behavior. As a student enters the classroom, you could say, "I noticed that you participated actively in your book club discussion yesterday, but you never interrupted the other book club members while they were talking. I was impressed." In addition to words of praise, you can show approval with nonverbal communication. Nods and smiles can be as effective as words. Jim Knight (2011) recommends that teachers practice the 3:1 ratio of praise to correction. After all, by only focusing on correction, you send a message that the only students who will get attention are those who do not meet expectations. Dr. Ethna Reid, after studying twenty years of data, concluded that reading teachers whose students achieved at the highest levels practiced a 3:1 ratio of positive to negative feedback (Jensen, 2013). Positive reinforcement makes the most impact!

As you incorporate more praise, consider how you deliver it. The praise should not be general in nature. If you say, "good job," the student only becomes motivated to please you, and this motivation is simply not sustainable. Instead, be specific. "I like how Jeremy got right to work on his online discussion this morning." "Kate showed remarkable creativity in her post when she proposed that students send editorials to the newspaper about the school funding legislation." Being specific helps learners know exactly what is working so they repeat the action or behavior.

I observed a highly effective teacher who found great success in asking students to be involved in praising other students' good behavior. Each morning, she gave six students the job of being "encouragers." It was a sought-after position in her classroom. The encouragers would take notes throughout the day regarding positive behaviors they witnessed. Then, at certain points, they would give *specific* praise to deserving students. The praise that students receive from their colleagues can be as motivating, if not more motivating, as praise from their teacher.

The best way for you to encourage positive behavior is to build relationships with your students. Learn about them as individuals. Talk to them about what they enjoy doing outside of school. Learn about their dreams and encourage those dreams. Students work for teachers who show they care!

A perfect blend of rewards and consequences is the key to a happy classroom culture that will be the foundation for learning.

Chapter Eight Summary

- ▶ In the Institute of Education Sciences 2010 report, the item that showed the highest correlation between teacher practice and reading achievement was teacher management and responsiveness.

- ▶ Carefully select appropriate lighting, items to hang on walls, and arrangement of furniture in order to create a space for optimal learning.

- ▶ Put into place specific procedures so that your classroom runs smoothly without opportunities for students to subvert you.

- ▶ A smile can cause a brain reaction that will help your students' learning.

- ▶ Give students a chance to build their classroom community by creating their own laws and classroom jobs.

- ▶ Provide a 3:1 ratio of reinforcement for positive behavior and consequences for behavior that negatively impacts learning.

CHAPTER NINE

A Sample Week in the Flipped Reading Block

At this point, you know the components to include in your reading block. Here is a condensed list:

- ▶ Flipped mini-lessons aligned to skills students need to practice and master

- ▶ Face-to-face follow-up mini-lessons that include time for students to practice with partners

- ▶ Opportunities for students to reflect online within strategy practice groups

- ▶ Teacher-guided meetings with strategy practice groups

- ▶ Opportunities for students to communicate online with members of a book club

- ▶ Opportunities for students to communicate face-to-face with members of book club

- ▶ Daily in-class reading (silent, with a partner, or while listening to a good reader)

- ▶ Reflective projects that are both independent and collaborative

- ▶ Long-term and short-term student goals and continual measurement of progress toward these goals with multiple types of assessment

- ▶ Movement integrated into student tasks

- ▶ A strong and positive classroom management system

By utilizing all these components of a flipped reading block, you will provide students with a variety of activities, flexible groupings, and opportunities for reading, writing, listening, speaking, creativity, collaboration, and critical thinking. You will also have great flexibility in the way you organize your reading block.

For this chapter, I have created a sample week based on a 58-minute reading block in a middle school classroom so that you can see one way to incorporate all the components. Of course, I would love for this reading block to be longer! In a report to the Carnegie Corporation, a panel of nationally known literacy experts recommended that middle school students spend two to four hours daily in reading-centered activities (Biancarosa & Snow, 2006). The reality, though, is that most reading blocks at the middle school and high school level are under an hour in length, so this example reflects the amount of time most teachers have in their reading blocks.

> ## A Student's Perspective
>
> " Learning in a variety of ways, using different media and experimenting with new methods and procedures, always makes learning fun and interesting. "
> —*Brittany, high-school student*

Please keep in mind that the writing I recommend in this book is designed to reinforce reading skills and to assist students in becoming reflective, active readers. While students engage in the writing on the discussion board, they will practice moving thoughts from their brains into text, and this will naturally increase their writing ability. However, students still need practice in all modes of writing, including narrative, descriptive, expository, and persuasive writing. In addition to the flipped reading block structure, a teacher will still need a structure, such as a writers' workshop, to support students in developing as writers.

I believe in keeping both a reading and a writing block at least through the end of middle school, and for some students, through the end of high school. However, I realize that many middle schools and high schools have one combined English/ language arts and reading period each day. Trying to teach reading, writing, listening, and speaking in only one period a day is no easy feat, but it can be done. For instance, since students write every day in the flipped reading block, a teacher may focus on reading for five days, then follow with two or three days of writers' workshop. During the writers' workshop days, the students might continue their at-home reading so that it will be easy to transition from a few days of writers' workshop back to five more days of the flipped reading block.

The week-long reading plan in this chapter demonstrates how you can blend online learning and face-to-face learning to create an engaging experience for students. Keep in mind that you have a great deal of flexibility with the flipped and blended reading approach. Depending on your access to technology, the length of your reading block, and the particular students you serve, you can adjust this structure to meet your students' needs.

Before you begin reading the lessons, let me give you some background information.

Knowing that integrating disciplines helps students make meaning, I have created a week of reading lessons that relate to social studies. For this particular scenario, let's say that I, as the reading teacher, have met with the social studies teacher, who is teaching about World War II and the Holocaust. Because our brains are designed to make connections, in my example unit, students will be reading nonfiction articles and historical fiction related to World War II and the Holocaust.

Let's also say that we are in the second week of the unit. In their book clubs, students have already created their norms and their deadlines for daily reading, and they have already begun having online and face-to-face discussions about their texts.

You now have all the background information for the sample week's activities. Watch them unfold.

MONDAY

Objective

To make inferences about characters based on textual evidence.

Before class

Students have watched the flipped mini-lesson, "Making Inferences About Characters Based on Textual Evidence" (from Chapter Two). They have also read an additional line of the poem, and as an accountability piece and formative assessment they have posted an inference about that line on the discussion board.

Opening class activity (7 minutes)

Students begin class in their independent learning formation.

Students write the lesson objective in their learning logs, along with academic and behavioral strategies that will help them meet the objective.

When they have finished, they silently read a short excerpt from Anne Frank's *Diary of a Young Girl*. After reading the excerpt, they write adjectives to describe Anne.

Whole class, face-to-face follow-up to the flipped mini-lesson (8 minutes)

Students begin this activity still in their independent learning formation.

The teacher guides students in a whole-group strategy lesson that requires active, collaborative learning. Students get up from their desks, and in fifteen silent seconds, each student finds a topic partner with whom to share their writing. They justify their adjectives about Anne with evidence from the text. The teacher walks around, listening to conversations. After three or four minutes, students have ten silent seconds to move back to their independent learning seats. The teacher carefully selects a few students who have demonstrated an understanding of supporting inference with text evidence to teach the whole class. The students then use the interactive whiteboard, on which the excerpt is projected, to highlight the textual evidence that supports the chosen adjectives. These students tell the rest of the class how they have supported their inferences with a mixture of background knowledge and evidence from the text.

Time for in-class, small-group reading (18 minutes total, including a two minute brain break).

Give students fifteen silent seconds to move their desks and themselves to their strategy practice group formation.

Brain break (2 minutes)

Today's follow-up to the mini lesson required students to tax their brains. Justifying inferences can be difficult for many students. Although there has been movement during the follow-up to the mini lesson, students would benefit from calming music and stretching to reframe their brains and prepare for reading.

Each strategy practice group will follow the brain-break leader in two minutes of stretching while the teacher plays music.

Small-group read-aloud, including pauses for inferences (16 minutes)

The teacher has found links to articles at varying reading levels about modern human rights struggles. Each of the four strategy practice groups has been assigned an article based on reading level. In small groups, students begin reading the articles. They take turns reading aloud or do a choral read, stopping every two paragraphs to summarize and make an inference. They write their inferences in the margins on digital sticky notes. If the classroom does not have devices that allow for digital note-taking, the teacher may choose to print the articles.

The teacher pulls one strategy practice group to the kidney table and reads aloud with them while the group follows along and whisper reads. She stops intermittently to ask students to reflect and make an inference supported by textual evidence and background knowledge. She has chosen this group because their formative assessments after the flipped lesson show that the members of this group are struggling with using textual evidence to support inferences. The teacher guides this group through the process of making inferences.

Whole-class, face-to-face mini-lesson (5 minutes)

Give students fifteen silent seconds to move their desks and themselves back to their independent learning formation.

The teacher shows an example of a student's discussion board post about making an inference. She asks students to talk with shoulder partners about how the student has backed his or her inference with a blend of background knowledge and textual evidence. After time to discuss with partners, the teacher brings the class back together with a five-second countdown. Then, she asks one student to highlight examples of textual evidence on the interactive whiteboard.

Brain break (1 minute)

Students stand by their desks and the entire class participates in a quick stretch, led by a student.

Reflection (14 minutes)

Students stay in their independent learning formation.

Students respond to a thread on their strategy practice group discussion board that requires them to write about a strategy used to make an inference in today's reading. After posting a response, each student writes a response to a colleague's post. When they finish this assignment, students may also post to one of the threads for their book club. Each learner can choose the thread that seems most meaningful at this particular point in the reading of the book club's book. For instance, a student may choose to write about a powerful passage, or to make a connection between the novel and another text. A student could also post an image related to the reading or ask a question. If students have enough time, they could create an online cartoon that adds a visual and shows dialogue between two characters. (See "Threads for Book Clubs" in Chapter Five for other examples of posts.) While students are working, the teacher pulls a second strategy practice group to the kidney table. This time, she pulls the highest ability group, which has read a very challenging article during the group reading time. She guides them through the making of an inference about the article.

Wrap-up (5 minutes)

Students remain in their independent learning formation.

- ▶ Student encouragers praise individual classmate's behavior.
- ▶ The teacher reviews the strategy for making an inference. She reminds students struggling with the article to watch the flipped mini-lesson again. She also assigns students to watch a second flipped mini-lesson on using context clues to determine word meaning in preparation for tomorrow's class.
- ▶ Students fill out self-assessment rubrics.
- ▶ Students follow appropriate procedures for putting away materials.

TUESDAY

Objectives:

- ▶ To make inferences about characters based on textual evidence.
- ▶ To determine word meaning through context clues.

Before class:

The students watch the flipped lesson and take a short online quiz on determining word meaning through context clues.

Opening class activity (5 minutes)

Students begin class in their independent learning formation.

Students add a new academic objective and behavior objective to their learning logs. Students read a second excerpt from Anne Frank's *Diary of a Young Girl*. They identify unknown words. If students are reading on electronic devices, they can highlight the words. If not, they can underline them on a hard copy or write them on sticky notes.

Whole class, face-to-face follow-up to the flipped mini-lesson (7 minutes)

Students begin this activity in their independent learning formation.

The teacher gives directions for students on the north side of the classroom to find a sitting partner on the south side of the classroom in fifteen silent seconds. (See Chapter Three for more guidance on standing/sitting pairs.) Partners look for synonyms and antonyms surrounding each unknown word to help them define it. After five minutes, the teacher gives directions for standing partners to move back to their independent work seats. Several students share their examples with the whole group by highlighting them on the interactive whiteboard.

Brain break (2 minutes)

Students stand by their desks, then must touch a door, a window, a wall, the floor, and the back of ten chairs before sitting back down.

Silent reading time (18 minutes)

The teacher dismisses one section of the classroom to move to comfortable spots for reading. Then, she dismisses a second section. Any students who did not make good choices the last time they chose their reading spots will stay in their independent seats for today's silent reading time.

Students finish reading and annotating yesterday's articles. Today, as they read silently, they look for inferences and underline unknown words. They also practice the strategy of determining word meaning through context clues. When students finish the article, they can read from their book club books.

While students are reading silently, the teacher pulls all students who were not successful on the online quiz to the kidney table. She guides them through the correct answers. Then, she sends them back to silent reading time and pulls a strategy practice group to the kidney table to work on determining word meaning through context clues.

Short spurt of talking time (3 minutes)

Students have ten silent seconds to move back to their independent formations.

Once students are back in their seats, the teacher gives instructions for the talking-with-a-partner activity. Then, with a shoulder partner, each student shares one example of the work he or she did on determining the word's meaning through context clues.

Reading response time (15 minutes)

Students remain in their independent learning formations.

Students submit posts on their strategy practice group discussion board. In the posts, they show how they determined a word's meaning using context clues. When they finish this assignment, students may post to one of their book club threads. (See "Threads for Book Clubs" in Chapter Five for ideas.)

While students are reflecting on their reading, the teacher pulls another strategy practice group to work with them on making inferences and determining word meaning. Over the past two days, the teacher has met with each strategy practice group once.

Meeting with book clubs (5 minutes)

Students have fifteen silent seconds to find their book club members for a quick, standing book club meeting. They move silently until they are standing back to back with their book club members. When the teacher sees that all students have found their groups, she says, "Turn and talk to your book club colleagues."

Students need this brief meeting with book clubs since, tomorrow, club members will meet face-to-face for a book club discussion. There are four discussion groups in this class. One is reading *Milkweed* (Spinelli, 2003). Another is reading *Daniel's Story* (Matas, 1993). A third is reading *Number the Stars* (Lowry, 1989). The final group is reading *The Devil's Arithmetic* (Yolen, 2004). Each book club's discussion leader reminds colleagues about their student-created assignments as to how many chapters should be read by tomorrow. The leader also reminds students to complete the student-determined number of posts and responses to threads.

Wrap-up (3 minutes)

- ▶ Students return to their independent learning formation.
- ▶ Student encouragers praise individual classmate's behavior.
- ▶ The teacher briefly reviews the strategies for making inferences and determining word meanings. She reminds students that they will take an online assessment on these skills on Friday.
- ▶ The homework assignment is given—to read and post on the discussion board in preparation for tomorrow's book club meeting.
- ▶ Students fill out self-assessment rubrics.
- ▶ Students follow appropriate procedures for putting away materials.

WEDNESDAY

Objectives:

▶ To make inferences about characters based on textual evidence.

▶ To determine word meaning through context clues.

▶ To make authentic connections to text.

Before the class

Before class, students have caught up on book club readings, submitted the required number of posts on the discussion board, and re-watched the flipped mini lessons if they needed a refresher on these skills in preparation for Friday's test.

Opening class activity (7 minutes)

Students begin class in their independent learning formation.

Students add additional academic and behavior goals to the learning log and demonstrate evidence of progress toward this week's academic and behavior goals.

Students silently read a third excerpt from Anne Frank's *Diary of a Young Girl.* Again, they look for opportunities to make inferences and to determine any unknown words using context clues.

Whole class, face-to-face follow-up to the flipped mini-lesson (8 minutes)

Students on the south side of the room have fifteen silent seconds to move to the north side of the room to find a sitting partner.

Using the text excerpt, students work with partners to make inferences about characters and determine unknown words using context clues. The teacher facilitates as necessary.

Preparation for book club meetings (5 minutes)

Students return to their independent learning formation.

Students take this short time to review posts and gather their thoughts before moving into the face-to-face book club meetings. While students are doing so, the teacher meets briefly with each discussion leader to look over questions the leader has created and to offer suggestions.

Book club meetings (18 minutes)

Students have fifteen silent seconds to move desks and themselves into their book club formation.

At this time, students may talk about anything they wish, as long as it is related to their books. The discussion leader will guide the discussion, but colleagues can bring up topics that they want to discuss. Although students may want to talk about strategies for reading, this is a time when they can also really think critically and talk about the life lessons they have learned from their books. Some groups may throw around a discussion ball to make sure each student gets uninterrupted speaking time. Some groups may use talking chips. Other groups may be able to maintain positive behaviors in the group without any of these behavioral support tools.

Brain break (2 minutes)

The book clubs follow the brain-break leaders in two minutes of movement before silent reading.

Silent reading (15 minutes)

Students have fifteen silent seconds to move desks and themselves back to the independent learning formation. Then, the teacher dismisses students in sections to find silent reading spots.

At this time, students have the choice either to read their book club books silently or to re-read the articles in which they made inferences and practice for Friday's assessment.

Wrap-up (3 minutes)

- ▶ Student encouragers praise individual classmate's behaviors.

- ▶ The teacher briefly reviews the strategies for making inferences and determining word meanings. She reminds students that they will take an online assessment on these strategies on Friday. The homework is given—read assigned chapters in their book club novels.

- ▶ Students fill out self-assessment rubrics.

- ▶ Students follow appropriate procedures for putting away materials.

THURSDAY

Objectives:

- ▶ To make inferences about characters based on textual evidence.

- ▶ To determine word meaning through context clues.

- ▶ To make authentic connections to text.

Opening activity (7 minutes)

Students begin class in their independent learning formation.

Students add evidence to show their progress toward the academic and behavior objectives in their learning logs. Students silently read another excerpt from Anne Frank's *Diary of a Young Girl*. Each student may choose whether to focus on inferences or on determining word meaning through context clues.

Whole class, face-to-face follow-up to the flipped mini-lessons (8 minutes)

The teacher gives students fifteen silent seconds to stand back-to-back with a topic partner. Once she sees that they have all found a partner, she tells them to turn and practice together.

Students again practice the skills of making inferences and determining word meaning through context clues by working with a standing topic partner. (See Chapter Three for more information on topic partners).

Strategy practice group poetry reading (20 minutes)

Students have fifteen silent seconds to move desks and themselves into their strategy practice group formation.

In strategy practice groups, students read aloud the poem "First They Came for the Jews" by Robert Niemoller. Since this is a poem that all strategy practice groups can access, all are reading the same text for this assignment. Groups work together to make an inference about Niemoller's feelings in the poem about his own character. The teacher provides scaffolding for any groups that need additional support. Some groups make the inference easier and faster than others. Groups that successfully make the inference read "The Burning of the Books" by Bertholdt Brecht. Again, they work on making an inference about why the author is angry that his book is not on the list to be burned. Not all groups will get to this second poem.

Brain break (2 minutes)

Each strategy practice group follows its brain-break leader in two minutes of movement before moving into the silent reading/discussion board portion of the period.

Options: Silent reading time/discussion board (18 minutes)

Students have fifteen silent seconds to move desks and themselves back to their independent learning formation. Then, the teacher dismisses students in sections to find comfortable reading spots.

Each student chooses whether to read silently in his or her book club book or post to the discussion board. If students have reached their book club reading goal for the day, they may instead read from an individually selected book. While students are working, the teacher pulls a strategy group to work on this week's skills.

Wrap-up (3 minutes)

➤ Students return to their independent learning formation.

➤ Student encouragers praise individual classmate's behaviors.

➤ The teacher briefly reviews the strategies for making inferences and determining word meanings. She reminds students that they will take an online assessment on these strategies tomorrow. The homework assignment is given—to study for the assessment (possibly re-watching the recorded mini-lessons), to read assigned chapters in book club novels, and to complete the required number of book club posts on the discussion board.

▶ Students fill out self-assessment rubrics.

▶ Students follow procedures for putting away materials.

FRIDAY

Assessment (16 minutes including one minute of stretching)

Students begin in their independent learning formation. A student leads the entire class in stretches before the assessment.

Students take a short online assessment about making inferences and determining word meaning using context clues. Students read two new short passages so that they can demonstrate that they are able to transfer the skills they have learned to a new text. If students finish early, they may review their book club's discussion board posts in preparation for the book club meetings.

Book club meetings (17 minutes, including two minutes of a brain break)

Students have fifteen silent seconds to move desks and themselves into book club formation.

Brain-break leaders lead the students in two minutes of exercise.

Discussion leaders then lead their groups in authentic discussions about their books. The teacher walks around, records data, and facilitates as needed. The discussion leaders also ask the group to begin thinking about ideas for a long-term collaborative project about the book.

Week's reflection and goal-setting (10 minutes)

Students have fifteen silent seconds to move desks and themselves back to the independent learning formation.

Student encouragers praise individual classmate's behaviors.

Using self-assessment rubrics for data, students reflect on their achievements and behaviors in learning logs. They record their progress toward academic and behavior goals. Based on this reflection, the students set goals for the coming week.

Movie viewing (15 minutes)

Because the class as a whole has exhibited positive independent and collaborative learning behaviors all week, they have earned fifteen minutes of a student choice activity. The students have voted for fifteen minutes of a movie. They have told the teacher that they have been reading about sad topics, so they want to watch

The Flipped Reading Block © 2015 by Gina Pasisis, Scholastic Teaching Resources

something funny. One student has found some World War II cartoons. The teacher has reviewed them for appropriateness, and the class will spend the final fifteen minutes watching the cartoons.

The teacher and students wish each other a happy weekend!

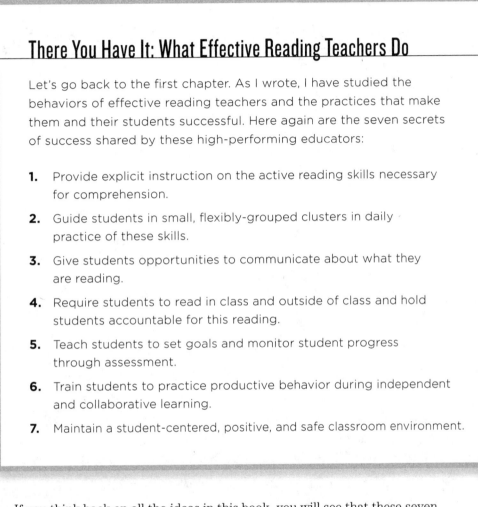

There You Have It: What Effective Reading Teachers Do

Let's go back to the first chapter. As I wrote, I have studied the behaviors of effective reading teachers and the practices that make them and their students successful. Here again are the seven secrets of success shared by these high-performing educators:

1. Provide explicit instruction on the active reading skills necessary for comprehension.

2. Guide students in small, flexibly-grouped clusters in daily practice of these skills.

3. Give students opportunities to communicate about what they are reading.

4. Require students to read in class and outside of class and hold students accountable for this reading.

5. Teach students to set goals and monitor student progress through assessment.

6. Train students to practice productive behavior during independent and collaborative learning.

7. Maintain a student-centered, positive, and safe classroom environment.

If you think back on all the ideas in this book, you will see that these seven secrets are embedded in every one. It is my wish that the flipped reading block approach will help your learners reach levels of success beyond what you can even imagine, and that it will create a structure for active reading and active learning that incorporates the 21st-century skills of communication, collaboration, critical thinking, and creativity.

May your teaching experience be as joyful has mine has been!

Discussion Board Writing Skeletons for Practicing What Skilled Readers Do

In Chapter Three, I listed what skilled readers do as they read. Here is that list again:

Skilled readers:

- ▶ .Set a purpose for their reading.

- ▶ Make use of text features and visuals to aid them in understanding the main text.

- ▶ Self-assess continually as they read. They check for understanding, reread, and use context clues to determine word meaning and make sense of complex text. They use word decoding strategies to determine the meanings of unknown words.

- ▶ Create a movie in their heads as they read. They make use of the author's language to visualize the text.

- ▶ Look for text patterns that aid in comprehension.

- ▶ Search for big ideas so they understand the author's message (main idea, purpose, and theme).

- ▶ Make connections between the text and their own lives, the text and the world, and the text and other texts. This constant synthesis of information while reading makes the reader actively engaged.

- ▶ Allow text to spark their natural intellectual curiosity, which leads to questions.

- ▶ Distinguish between essential and non-essential ideas in text.

- ▶ Separate fact from opinion. They are discerning consumers of textual information

- ▶ Make inferences, draw conclusions, and make predictions based on text evidence.

- ▶ Analyze an author's literary elements and techniques as a way to enhance understanding and appreciation of text.

(Diamond, L., Honig, B. & Gutlohn, L. , 2013; Duke, N. & Pearson, P., 2002; Duke, N., Pearson, P., Strachan, S. & Billman, A., 2011; Wilhelm, 2001)

This appendix gives a prompt for a thread, an example of a discussion board writing skeleton, and a writing example to align with each of these skills. A pdf of the writing skeletons and examples is available online; see page 154 for details on how to access.

SET A PURPOSE FOR READING

Prompt for discussion board thread:

What is your purpose for reading [name story, article, or book]?

Writing skeleton:

My purpose for reading [name article, story, poem, or book] is to [state purpose or goal].

Example:

My purpose for reading "Turn on Creativity" is to learn ways to spark my own creativity. To do this, I will continually pause throughout the article and ask, "What are the significant ideas presented in the article and how can I apply these in my own life?"

USE TEXT FEATURES

Prompt for discussion board thread:

Write about the text features of your story, article, or book. Connect them to your prior knowledge, and then predict what your story, article, or book will be about.

Writing skeleton:

Before I began reading today, I looked at the title, [name the title], and the headings, [name the headings]. Then, I looked at the illustrations, which depicted [describe the illustrations]. I connected the text features to my prior knowledge. [Explain the connection.] After analyzing the text features, I predicted that this story would be about [write about the prediction].

Example:

Before I began reading today, I looked at the title, *Through My Eyes* (Bridges, 1999), and the headings, "Born in the Deep South," "One Year in an All Black School," "November 14, 1960," "The First Day at William Frantz," "My First White Teacher," "Riots in New Orleans," and "The End of First Grade." Then, I looked at the illustrations, which depicted protesters holding signs that read "We want segregation" and an African-American child walking between deputy U.S. Marshalls. I also saw photographs of hooded Ku Klux Klan members standing in front of a burning cross. I connected the text features to my prior knowledge. From the headings, it is clear that the story takes place in the South in 1960 and has something to do with schools. The picture of Ku Klux Klan members shows me that this book is about racism. The illustrations show protesters fighting against integration and U.S. Marshalls protecting a child. After analyzing the text structures, I predict that this story will be about an African-American child who tries to go to a school for white children.

Alternate text feature skeletons:

As I [explain information you looked up or analyzed], I studied the [name text feature—glossary, table of contents, index, map, picture, margin guide, chart, diagram, table, graph]. This helped me [write about your discovery].

SELF-ASSESSMENT

Prompt for discussion board thread:

How did you self-assess as you were reading, and what strategy or strategies did you use to improve your comprehension?

Writing skeleton:

As I was reading, I became confused when [explain what was happening in the text]. To help myself understand this confusing part, I [explain the strategy used to improve comprehension].

Example:

As I was reading *The Giver* (Lowry, 1993), I became confused when the announcer said that the training pilot would be released for making a mistake. I could not understand the meaning of the word "released" in this context. To help myself understand the confusing part, I reread the section that I did not understand. I read slowly, and I paused after each paragraph to make sure that I could make sense of every part of the text. After reading the text, I determined that the author did not intend for me to understand yet what the word "released" means. Instead, she wants for me to make guesses. I made a guess that whatever it means to be released is not something anyone would want. It can't be positive because being released is the society's reaction to behavior that was not in line with society's expectations.

Alternate self-assessment skeleton:

Today, I lost my focus when [explain]. The way I got back on track was [explain].

USE CONTEXT TO DETERMINE THE MEANING OF WORDS

Prompt for discussion board thread:

Explain how you used context clues to find the meaning of an unknown word.

Writing skeleton:

I encountered the interesting word, [insert word here]. I found its meaning by using context clues. The word is in the following sentence: "[Write the sentence]." I used a context clue to determine the meaning. [Explain the clue used]. That led me to understand that the word [insert word here] means [insert definition or synonym here].

Example:

I encountered the interesting word, "tenaciously." I found its meaning by using context clues. The word was in the following sentence: "The dog sank his jaws into my knee and held on tenaciously until a gun fired, signaling the dog to give up and let go." I used a context clue to determine the meaning of the word. Since it took something as intense as the firing of a gun to make the dog stop, that led me to understand that the word "tenaciously" means not giving up.

USE WORD DECODING STRATEGIES

Prompt for discussion board thread:

Explain how you used a word decoding strategy to determine the meaning of an unknown word.

Writing skeleton:

I did not understand the word [write the word], so I broke it apart. The prefix, [write the prefix], means [write prefix definition]. The root, [write the root], means [write root definition]. Putting those definitions together, I can decode the word [write the word] to determine it means [write meaning].

Example:

I did not understand the meaning of the word *midfield*, so I broke it apart. The prefix, *mid-*, means *middle*. The root, *field*, means an area of open land. Putting these definitions together, I can decode the word, midfield, to mean the middle of a field. Because I am reading a book about soccer, I can determine that the word is about the middle point between goals.

VISUALIZE TEXT

Prompt for discussion board thread:

Explain how you visualized what you read.

Writing skeleton:

While I was reading, I created a movie in my head. In [name text] when [name author] [summarize portion of text], I imagined [describe what you imagined].

Example:

While I was reading, I created a movie in my head. In the excerpt from *The House on Mango Street* (Cisneros, 1991), when Sandra Cisneros compares Grandpa's fat feet to thick tamales, I imagined Grandpa struggling to push his plump feet into his brown leather shoes. I also imagined Grandma's awkward gait as I read Cisneros's descriptions of the character wearing high heels in which she could not walk without wobbling.

Alternate visualization skeletons:

Today, I created a picture in my head. When the author writes that "[provide quote]," I imagined this: [draw the picture, capture the image with a tablet or smart phone, and attach it to the discussion board post].

FIND A PATTERN IN A TEXT

Prompt for discussion board thread:

What pattern did you find in the text? Why do you think the author decided to use this pattern?

Writing skeleton:

In my reading of [name text], I noticed that [the author] arranged the events in [chronological order, order of cause/effect, order of most important to least important]. I think [he or she] decided on this arrangement because [explain why].

Example:

In my reading of "The Night the Bed Fell on Father"(Thurber, 1945), I noticed that Thurber arranged the events in chronological order. I think he decided on this arrangement because each event built on the one before it to cause mass confusion, which resulted in a household filled with hysterical people, even though a reason for hysteria did not exist. The hilarious story needed to be organized chronologically so that the reader could understand how each character reacted to a misunderstanding about the actions of another character.

Alternate pattern skeletons:

In my reading today, I found an example of [chronological order, cause/effect, order of most important to least important]. [Write about that example].

DETERMINE MAIN IDEA

Prompt for discussion board thread:

How did you determine the main idea of the passage?

Writing skeleton:

In the excerpt from [name the text], I determined the main idea. Throughout the passage, [write about the recurring idea]. [Give examples of the way the idea appears in the beginning, middle, and end of the passage.]

Example:

In the excerpt from *Bud, Not Buddy* (Curtis, 1999), I determined the main idea. Throughout the passage, the author, Curtis, writes that libraries have a hypnotizing smell. In the beginning of the passage, Curtis describes the smell of old books, using the adjectives "soft, drowsy, and powdery." In the middle of the passage, he describes how people fall asleep from the smell when the smelly powder weighs down eyelids. At the end, he writes about "tossing out drooly folks," who have been lured into a smell-induced sleep. Since the hypnotizing smell idea is in the beginning, middle, and end, I know it is the main idea.

INTERPRET THE AUTHOR'S PURPOSE

Prompt for discussion board thread:

How did you determine the author's purpose of the text?

Writing skeleton:

In my reading of [name the literature] today, the author's purpose became quite clear. [Write about the part of the text that reveals the author's purpose].

Example:

In my reading of *Eleanor Roosevelt* (Freedman, 1991) today, the author's purpose became quite clear. The author writes about Eleanor's difficulty as a child. She had a mother who did not show her affection and who told her she was ugly. Yet, Eleanor loved her mother intensely, and she grieved over her mother's death. After this devastating childhood experience, even more tragedy would befall her. Her beloved father succumbed to the ravages of alcoholism-related disease, and he died, too. Not only did Eleanor endure the pain of losing both parents, but she then had to live with an abusive grandmother, who forced her to take cold baths and refrain from talking during meals. Despite all of this heartache, she remained strong and became a woman who would fight for the disenfranchised and economically marginalized. The author's purpose is to show that the human spirit is stronger than any of life's adversities.

IDENTIFY THEME

Prompt for discussion board thread:

How did you determine the theme of the passage?

Writing skeleton:

One of the themes of [name story, poem, article, or novel] is [write the theme]. The author supports the theme with [provide textual evidence to support the theme].

Example:

One of the themes of "Tom Sawyer Whitewashing the Fence," a chapter from *The Adventures of Tom Sawyer* (Twain, 2008), is that people most desire the things most difficult to acquire. When Tom Sawyer hesitates to let his friend, Ben, try a few strokes of whitewashing, Ben becomes very interested in the task. Eventually, Ben begins to beg and finally, he offers Tom an apple for the chance to paint. When the other boys find out that Ben has paid for the opportunity, they want in on the action, too. Each one offers some form of payment, from a kite to a dead rat and a string to swing it with. At the end of the chapter, Twain cements the theme. If a task costs money, people desire to do it and consider it fun.

Alternate theme skeletons:

- A major theme of my [book/poem/article/story] is [write about theme]. In my reading today, I noticed that the character, [name of character], reinforced this theme by [write about what the character says or does to reinforce the theme].

- A theme of my [book/poem/article/story] is [write about theme]. I have encountered this theme before in [name text]. That multiple authors write about this same theme tells me that [explain what this means to you].

 The Flipped Reading Block © 2015 by Gina Pasisis, Scholastic Teaching Resources

- During my reading today of [title], I learned a valuable lesson. I learned [explain the lesson]. Next time I encounter [explain a situation in which the lesson will be valuable], I will [explain what you will do] because [tell why].

MAKE TEXT-TO-SELF CONNECTIONS

Prompt for discussion board thread:

What text-to-self connections did you make?

Writing skeleton:

The author of the autobiography I am reading has had life experiences to which I can relate. In [title of text], [describe the author's experience]. Like [author's name], I, too, have [explain your experience].

Example:

The author of the autobiography I am reading has had life experiences to which I can relate. In "Punch Brothers Punch" (Twain, 1876), Mark Twain describes how a jingle from an advertisement stuck in his head. He describes his torment as he tries unsuccessfully to break free of the annoying, but very catchy advertisement. In his head, he hears the jingle over and over until he is driven near to madness by it. I laughed at this because I guess a fine line exists between comedy and pain. Like Twain, I, too, have gotten a song stuck in my head. Once, I earned a bad grade on a test because I couldn't concentrate on the test while the words and music of the song, "Over There," played over and over in my brain. This connection makes me think: Is a painful experience always what is under the surface of writing that is funny?

Alternate text-to-self skeletons:

- A character in my [article, story, poem, or book] has life experiences to which I relate. In [name the text], [describe the character's or person's experience]. Like [character's/person's name], I, too, have [explain your experience].

- In my reading of [title] today, I identified with [name of character or person], who showed that [he or she] feels [explain feeling]. I identified with this because [explain]. This feeling is, in fact, universal because many people [explain why other people share this feeling].

- The character [name of character] reminds me of [person who shares characteristics]. First, [explain the similarity]. Also, [explain another similarity].

- Before reading [name text], I [write about prior knowledge that helped you understand the text]. This prior knowledge helped me understand the text because [explain why].

- My novel's character, [name], values [what he or she values]. I share this thinking because I feel that [explain why].

- My novel's character, [name], values [what he or she values]. I do [share/do not share] this thinking because I feel that [explain why].

- The text I read today, [title], changed my perspective on [state the issue or idea]. Before, I believed that [explain prior belief]. Now, I believe [explain new belief].

- In the passage I read today from [title], the author, [author name], explores the theory of [explain theory]. A different author, [author's name], does not share this belief. Instead, [he or she] believes that [explain theory]. I agree with [author's name] because [explain why].

- The character I read about today in [title] experiences relationship problems because [explain]. I have had similar problems with [name the person]. The best way to solve these problems is [state idea]. The reason this will work is [explain why].

MAKE TEXT-TO-SOCIETY CONNECTIONS

Prompt for discussion board thread:

What text-to-society connections did you make?

Writing skeleton:

Maybe it is true that art reflects life. As I read [title] today, I thought of a situation in the world that mirrors one in my book. Just like [describe the situation in the book], many people in [specific location in the world] also [describe the situation].

Example:

Maybe it is true that art reflects life. As I read *The Outsiders* (S. E. Hinton) today, I thought of a situation in the world that mirrors one in my book. Just like the battling Greasers and Socs, many people in the Middle East also find themselves as part of groups in conflict with other groups. The Israelis and the Palestinians represent large groups of people fighting for dominance over one another. Although the gangs in the book fight on a much smaller scale than the Israelis and Palestinians, the outcomes of the fighting are the same. The high cost of the conflict comes in the form of lost human lives and lost human spirit. Why do humans always fight with each other?

Alternate text-to-society skeletons:

One of the customs of the characters in my book is [name custom]. Like the characters in [name book], people in [name place] have similar customs. [Explain similarity].

The Flipped Reading Block © 2015 by Gina Pasisis, Scholastic Teaching Resources

MAKE TEXT-TO-TEXT OR TEXT-TO-MEDIA CONNECTIONS

Prompt for discussion board thread:

What text-to-text or text-to-media connections did you make?

Writing skeleton:

The excerpt from [name the article, story, poem, or book] that I read today reminds me of a scene from a movie [or play] that I saw. When [describe the situation in the text], I immediately thought of the scene from [name the movie or play]. In that scene, [describe the similar situation]. The difference was [describe the difference].

Example:

The excerpt from *The Watsons Go to Birmingham—1963* (Curtis, 1995) that I read today reminds me of a scene from a movie I saw. When Kenny earns the respect of his teenaged brother Byron by saving Joetta, I immediately thought about a scene from the movie *Home Alone*. *Home Alone*'s Kevin, like Kenny, suffers at the hands of a big brother who cannot see past his young age to realize that Kevin really has extraordinary inner strength. It is only after Kevin manages to protect the family home from a robbery by outwitting the bad guys that the older brother sees it. Making this connection makes me wonder: Is the dynamic between Kenny and his teenaged brother Byron typical? The difference is that Kenny saves a person and Kevin saves a thing.

Alternate text-to-text or text-to-media connections:

- The book excerpt that I read today made me think of another book [or story] that I have read. When [describe the situation in the book], I immediately thought of the scene from [name the second book or story]. In that scene, [describe the similar situation]. The one difference was [describe the difference].

- The character [name of character] in [title] reminds me of [name of character] from [name of book, movie, story, or play]. First, [explain the similarity]. Also, [explain another similarity].

ASK QUESTIONS

Prompt for discussion board thread:

What questions did you ask during your reading of the text?

Writing skeleton:

Today as I read [name the book], I thought of several questions. When I read about [describe the situation], I wondered, "[write a question]."

Example:

Today as I read *Where the Broken Heart Still Beats* (Meyer, 1992), I thought of several questions. It tells the story of Cynthia Ann Parker. When I read about her being captured as a child and taken in by Comanches after a raid, only to be recaptured and taken back into her old society as an adult, I wondered, "What type of person would enjoy reading this book?" Because of the content of the book, the type of person who would enjoy reading it would be someone who is curious about how early Americans struggled because this historical fiction reveals struggles not only of pioneers who traveled west, but also of Native Americans who tried desperately to hold on to their way of life.

DISTINGUISH BETWEEN ESSENTIAL AND NONESSENTIAL DETAILS

Prompt for discussion board thread:

Explain the central idea of the passage and then give examples of essential supporting ideas.

Writing skeleton:

In today's reading [title], the author's main point was [explain the central idea]. The author supports this point by [give examples of supporting ideas].

Example:

In today's reading, "Environmental Toxins Harm Children," the author's main point was to expose the problems that occur when government does not regulate industrial plants that produce environmental pollution. The author supports this point by showing how the main character, Dahlia, suffers from asthma. It is no coincidence that she lives by an industrial plant known to release dangerous toxins. The author also supports this point in the part of the article in which the owner of the plant says, "I don't care about children with asthma. They will eventually suffer from lung disease anyway because they will start smoking."

Other supporting detail skeletons:

In today's reading, [title], two details support the main idea. First, [write about the main idea and a supporting detail]. Also, [write about another detail]. Not all of the details directly supported the main idea. [Describe details that do not support the main idea, and tell why the author may have included these details even though they do not serve the purpose of supporting the main idea].

The Flipped Reading Block © 2015 by Gina Pasisis, Scholastic Teaching Resources

DISTINGUISH BETWEEN FACT AND OPINION IN TEXT

Prompt for discussion board thread:

Describe a fact or opinion you found in your reading.

Writing skeleton:

I found a [fact or opinion] in [name of book or article]. [Write the fact or opinion]. I know it is a [fact or opinion] because [explain why].

Example:

I found an opinion in Edmund Morris's *Colonel Roosevelt* (2010). The opinion is that, in 1910, Theodore Roosevelt was the most famous man in the world. I know it is an opinion because Morris does not reveal that this statement has been tested or proven. Morris does not back the statement up with a world-wide survey comparing Roosevelt to other very famous people of the time, such as King George V, Thomas Edison, or the Wright Brothers. I have no doubt that Theodore Roosevelt was famous. No one would argue that. However, to claim that he was "the most famous" is simply an opinion.

Writing skeleton:

I found a fact in [name of article or book]. [Write the fact]. I know it is a fact because [explain why].

Example:

I found a fact in "Harry Potter Grows Up." The author writes that the Harry Potter series is "wildly popular" (Goldberg, 2014). I know it is a fact because around 400 million Harry Potter books have sold.

Alternate fact/opinion skeletons:

- Through his (or her) writing, [author's name] shows that [he or she] believes that [explain the author's opinion]. [Provide textual evidence to support the claim that you have made about the author]. I agree (or disagree) with this opinion because [explain why].

- The author of the passage I read today explicitly asserts that [state assertion]. [He or she] supports this assertion by [explain support]. I believe [or do not believe] this because [explain why].

- The author of the passage I read today implicitly asserts that [state assertion] when [explain character's words or actions that support this]. I believe (or do not believe) this because [explain why].

MAKE INFERENCES/DRAW CONCLUSIONS SUPPORTED BY EVIDENCE

Prompt for discussion board thread:

Make an inference or draw a conclusion supported by evidence from the text.

Writing skeleton:

In [name the article, story, poem, or book], [name of character or person] [describe action]. I think [he or she] does this because [explain why]. The action is morally right (or morally wrong) because [explain why].

Example:

In *Harry Potter and the Sorcerer's Stone* (Rowlings, 1999), Aunt Marge tells Harry that he hasn't been beaten hard enough because of the casual way he talks about the beatings. I think she does this because of her cold and heartless attitude toward this orphan. After all, despite Harry Potter's power, he is a victim of abuse. Her action is morally wrong because she should be his protector, not someone who permits him to suffer at the hands of another.

Other inference skeletons:

In [name the book], a character, [name of character], [describe action]. I think [he or she] does this because [explain why]. The action is wise (or foolish) because [explain why].

MAKE PREDICTIONS

Prompt for discussion board thread:

What ideas in the text caused you to make a prediction?

Writing skeleton:

I encountered some ideas that I feel I must keep in mind as I continue to read [title of text]. [Explain idea and its importance]. I must keep these ideas in mind because [write what you predict].

Example:

I encountered some ideas that I feel I must keep in mind as I continue to read "Kid Chefs at the White House" (Chambers, 2014). The author points out that all children who entered the contest must create recipes and prepare food that meets the My Plate guidelines, which encourage a healthy balance of protein, starches, vegetables, and dairy. I must keep these ideas in mind because I predict that the winners, who will be discussed later in the article, will have prepared meals that include this healthy balance.

Other prediction skeletons:

Before I read this passage from my novel [title], I predicted that [prediction]. I made this prediction because [explain reason]. What actually happens is [write what happens in the passage].

ANALYZE LITERARY ELEMENTS: SETTING

Prompt for discussion board thread:

What is the setting of the story and why is this setting important?

Writing skeleton:

[Name article, story, poem or book title] takes place in [name place]. It reminds me of [name real place in world] because [explain why]. The setting is important in the story because [explain importance].

Example:

To Kill a Mockingbird (Lee, 1960), takes place in a fictional place called Maycomb, Alabama. It makes me think of my grandparent's small town in Illinois because in Maycomb there are few newcomers and the people who live there typically have generations of ancestors who have lived there. This is true of my grandparent's small town, as well. No one new arrives because there is no big industry to attract them. People often stay, though, because of family businesses or just the simple fear of change. *To Kill a Mockingbird* is set during the 1930s. The setting is important in the story because it is a period before the Civil Rights Movement. It was a period in which racism was monstrous and unchecked. Because of the setting, the reader can understand the historical context behind the town's treatment of Tom Robinson.

Alternate setting skeletons:

Even though the author does not explicitly state the setting, I can tell it is in [place] during [time period] because of [textual evidence].

ANALYZE LITERARY ELEMENTS: CONFLICT

Prompt for discussion board thread:

What is the conflict of the story?

Writing skeleton:

In [text I am reading], the main conflict [explain conflict].

Example:

In Gail Levine's novel, *Ella Enchanted* (1997), the main conflict occurs because the main character, Ella, was given a gift of obedience by a fairy, causing her to be unable to say no to anyone's command. This leads to conflict when her father remarries after her mother's death. Ella, a Cinderella-like figure, becomes the victim of a scheming stepmother and two ruthless stepsisters when they discover that she cannot refuse a command. Ella sees her only hope of resolving this conflict by breaking the spell.

Skeletons for climax and resolution:

- In [the text I am reading], the climax occurs when [explain].

- In [the text I am reading], the resolution of the conflict happens when [explain].

ANALYZE LITERARY ELEMENTS: CHARACTER

Prompt for discussion board thread:

Describe the development of a character.

Writing skeleton:

One of my novel's characters, [name of character], has developed considerably. At the beginning of the book [title], [name of character] is [adjective]. [He or she] [provide textual evidence to support the descriptive word]. Slowly, though, I began to notice a change. For instance, [provide textual evidence to support the claim that the character changed]. In the chapter I have just read, [provide textual evidence to support further development of the character]. Because of [explain the cause of the change], [name of character] has developed into a character who [describe the character at your current point in the book].

Example:

One of my novel's characters, Ivan, has developed considerably. At the beginning of the book, *The One and Only Ivan*, the gorilla thinks he is happy with his life. Eating bananas and doing artwork is enough for him. Slowly, though, I began to notice a change. For instance, when he sees Ruby get abused, he realizes that the Big Top Mall is not a good place to be. In the chapter I just read, he starts thinking of ways he can use his finger paints to paint pictures for the billboard so that people will get mad about the treatment of animals at the Big Top Mall. Because Ivan watches the suffering of Ruby, he has developed into a character who can't be happy with his current home and who wants to make a change.

Alternate characterization skeleton:

- In today's reading of [title], the author used the words, [write words], to describe the character, [name of character]. These words were very important because [explain importance of words].

- The main character of [title], [name], is [adjective]. I can see this when [he or she] says, "[Dialogue]."

- The main character of [title], [name], is [adjective]. [He or she] shows this when [he or she] [explain action].

ANALYZE LITERARY ELEMENTS

Literary techniques:

(rhyme, repetition, alliteration, poetic meter, onomatopoeia, hyperbole, dialogue, tone, paradox, satire, imagery, figurative language, simile, metaphor, sensory detail, symbol, personification, pun, idioms, irony, foreshadowing, oxymoron, paradox, etc.)

Prompt for discussion board thread:

How did the author's use of a literary technique affect your reading?

Writing skeleton:

As I read [name of author and text], I noticed that the author uses specific words and phrases to [explain how the author's craft affects the reading experience]. When I read the words, "[write words here]," I created a picture [or movie] in my head of [describe your picture or movie].

Example:

As I read O'Dell's *Island of the Blue Dolphins* (1988) I noticed that the author uses specific words and phrases to help me create a mental image of text. When I read the words that described the ship changing from a small shell to a gull with folded wings, I created a movie in my head of the ship growing in size as it moved closer. Now, I see the power of the simile!

Technology Terms

Asynchronous: the use of online learning tools to permit students to learn without the limitations of time and place

Blended learning: a blend of both online and face-to-face learning experiences

Chat tool: a web-based application that allows online communication

Digital immigrant: a person who was born before the age of digital technology

Digital native: a person who was born into the age of digital technology

Discussion board: an online forum where people can create a discussion by posting messages

DVD: a digital video disc

Flip cam: a small video camera

Flipped classroom: a model in which the teacher "flips" the traditional approach of lecture in class and homework at home by creating a video that provides the lecture for students to watch at home so class time can be spent on the active learning while the teacher facilitates and works with small groups

Interactive whiteboard: an interactive touch board that displays a computer's desktop

Learning management system: a web-based application used to set up and assess an educational course or program

Online whiteboard: an online blank space where one can draw or write for others to see

Screencast: a video recording of a the actions displayed on a computer

Screen shot: a single picture recording the items displayed on a computer screen

Smartphone: a mobile phone with many capabilities, including image and videos capture, communication through text and e-mail, and online access to information

Thread: string of related ideas exchanged among members of a discussion group on an online discussion board

USB drive: a small device that is used for data storage

Virtual learning: an online system of learning that models in-person education

Web Quest: an inquiry-based project that allows students to explore information online

Wiki: a website where users can add, change, and delete content

How to Access Downloadable Print Resources and View Online Videos

Go to teacherexpress.scholastic.com/flipped-reading-block to access the following resources.

Downloadable Print Resources

Technology Tools for the Flipped Reading Block: An Annotated List of Resources

Discussion Board Writing Skeletons

Online Videos

Tour of Edmodo Learning Management System

Model Flipped Mini-Lessons

- ▶ Making Inferences
- ▶ Finding the Main Idea
- ▶ Using a Test-Taking Strategy
- ▶ Analyzing Literary Techniques

Classroom Videos

- ▶ Classroom Tour
- ▶ Book Club Discussions
- ▶ Strategy Practice Group Sessions
- ▶ Whole-Group Guide Practice Activities
- ▶ Independent Routines in Action
- ▶ Movement Routine in Action
- ▶ Positive Culture in Action

References

Anderson, L. W., Krathwohl, D. R., Airasian, P. W., Cruikshank, K. A., Mayer, R. E., Pintrich, P. R., Raths, J., & Wittrock, M. C. (2001). *A taxonomy for learning, teaching, and assessing: A revision of Bloom's taxonomy of educational objectives.* New York: Pearson, Allyn & Bacon.

Applegate, K. & Castelao, P. (2012). *The one and only Ivan.* New York: HarperCollins Children's Books.

Bergmann, J., & Sams, A. (2012). *Flip your classroom: Reach every student in every class every day.* Alexandria, Virginia: ASCD.

Bernard, S. (2010, December 1). Science shows making lessons relevant really matters. In What Works in Education: The George Lucas Educational Foundation. Retrieved from http://www.edutopica.org/nueroscience-brain-based-learning-relevance-improves-engagement.

Biancarosa, C., & Snow, C. E. (2006). *Reading next—A vision for action and research in middle and high school literacy: A report to Carnegie Corporation of New York* (2nd ed.). Washington, DC: Alliance for Excellent Education.

Blumenthal, K. (2012). *Steve Jobs: The man who thought different.* New York: Feiwal and Friends.

Boushey, G. & Moser, J. (2006). *The daily five: Fostering literacy independence in the elementary grades.* Portland, ME: Stenhouse Publishers.

Brecht, B. (1995). The burning of the books. In Hilda Shiff (Ed.), *Holocaust poetry* (p. 9). New York: St. Martin's Press.

Bridges, R. (1999). *Through my eyes.* New York: Scholastic.

Chambers, R. (2014, July 14). Kid chefs at the White House. In *Time for Kids.* Retrieved from http://www.timeforkids.com/news/kid-chefs-white-house/167466.

Cisneros, S. (1991). *The house on Mango Street.* New York: Vintage Books.

Coleman, S. (n.d). Why do students like online learning? University of Maryland Baltimore County. Retrieved on March 3, 2015 from www.umbc.edu/isd/whyonlinelearning.html.

Curtis, C. (1999). *Bud, not Buddy*. New York: Delacorte Press.

Curtis, C. (1995). *The Watsons go to Birmingham—1963*. New York: Bantam Doubleday.

Daniels, H. (2002). *Literature circles: Voice and choice in book clubs and reading groups*. Portland, ME: Stenhouse Publishers.

Daniels, H. & Steineke, N. (2004). *Mini-lessons for literature circles*. Portsmouth, NH: Heinemann.

Dale, E. (1946). *Audio-visual methods in teaching*. New York: The Dryden Press.

Davis, B. H., Resta, V., Davis, L., & Camacho, A. (2001). Novice teachers learn about literature circles through collaborative action research. *Journal of Reading Education*. In Auger, T. (2003, May). Student-centered reading: A review of the research on literature circles. *EPS Update*.

Diamond, J., & Gaier, M. (2014). *Literacy lessons for a digital world*. New York: Scholastic.

Diamond L., Honig, B., & Gutlohn, L. (2013). *Teaching reading sourcebook (updated second edition)*. Novato, CA: Arena Press.

Dorhout, L. (2013, April 8). Personal interview at TAGT conference.

"Do you know? Ten things everyone should know about K–12 students' views on digital learning." (2012). In *Speak Up 2012 National Research Project Findings*. Retrieved from http://www.tomorrow.org/speakup/DLD2013_top10.html

Draper, S. M. (2010). *Out of my mind*. New York, NY: Athenum Books for Young Readers.

Duke, N., & Pearson, P. (2002). Effective practices for developing reading comprehension. In A. E. Farstrup & S. J. Samuels (Eds.), *What research has to say about reading instruction* (3rd ed., 205–242). Newark, DE: International Reading Association.

Duke, N., Pearson, P., Strachan, S., & Billman, A. (2011). Essential elements of fostering and teaching reading comprehension. In A.E. Farstrup & S. J. Samuels (Eds.), *What research has to say about reading instruction* (4th ed., 51–93). Newark, DE: International Reading Association.

Dunn, R. & Griggs, S. A. (Eds.). (2004). *Synthesis of the Dunn and Dunn learning-style model research: Who, what, when, where, and so what?* New York: St. John's University's Center for the Study of Learning and Teaching Styles. Early warning! Why reading by the end of third grade matters. (2010).

In *New York council on children and families.* Retrieved from http://ccf.ny.gov/KidsCount/kcResources/AECFReporReadingGrade3.pdf

Early warning! Why reading by the end of third grade matters. (2010). In *New York council of children and families.* Retrieved from http://ccf.ny.gov/KidsCount/kcResources/AECFReporReadingGrade3.pdf

Fay, J. & Funk, D. (1995). *Teaching with love and logic: Taking control of the classroom.* Golden, CO: The Love and Logic Press.

Fisher, D. & Frey, N. (2007). Implementing a schoolwide literacy framework: Improving achievement in an urban elementary school. *The Reading Teacher, 61*, pp. 32–45.

Fisher, D., & Frey, N. (2003). Writing instruction for struggling adolescent readers: A gradual release model. In *Journal of Adolescent and Adult Literacy, 46*, 396–407.

Fountas, I. & Pinnell G. S. (1996). *Guided reading: A good first teaching for all children.* Portsmouth, NH: Heinemann.

Frank, A. (1993). *The diary of a young girl.* New York: Bantam.

Freeman, H. (2012, August 25). Getting lost in a good book can help keep you healthy. In *The Daily Mail.* Retrieved from http://www.dailymail.co.uk/health/article-2193496/Getting-lost-good-book-help-healthy.html.

Freedman, R. (1991). *Eleanor Roosevelt: A life of discovery.* New York: Houghton Mifflin.

Friedman, T. L. (2005). *The world is flat: A brief history of the twenty-first century.* New York: Farrar, Straus and Giroux.

Gallagher, K. (2009). *Readicide: How schools are killing reading and what you can do about it.* Portland, ME: Stenhouse Publishers.

Gay, M. (2009). *Brain breaks for the classroom.* New York: Scholastic.

Goldberg, E. (2014, July 9). Harry Potter grows up. In *Time for Kids.* Retrieved from http://www.timeforkids.com/news/harry-potter-grows/167071.

Green, G. (2012, January 18). My view: Flipped classrooms give every student a chance to succeed. In *CNN.* Retrieved from http://schoolsofthought.blogs.cnn.com/2012/01/18/my-view-flipped-classrooms-give-every-student-a-chance-to-succeed/

Hinton, S. E. (1967). *The outsiders.* New York: Penguin Group.

Howard, V. (2009, October). Most of the books I've read, I've found on the floor: Teens and pleasure reading. *VOYA.*

Hughes, L. (1994) "Mother to Son." In *The Collected Poems of Langston Hughes.* New York: Vintage Books.

Iskander, M. (2011). A physical education in Naperville. In *Need to Know* on PBS.

James-Burdumy, S., Deke, J., Lugo-Gil, J. Carey, N., Hershey, A., Gersten, R., Newman-Gonchar, R., Dimino, J., & Haymond, K. (2010). Effectiveness of selected supplemental reading comprehension interventions: Findings from two student cohorts—Executive summary (NCEE 2010-4016). Washington, DC: National Center for Education Evaluation and Regional Assistance, Institute of Education Sciences, U.S. Department of Education.

Jensen, E. (2013, June 26–29). Teaching with Poverty in Mind Conference. Presented at Omni Conference Center, San Antonio, Texas.

Johnston, T. (2004). *The harmonica.* Watertown, MA: Charlesbridge.

Krashen, S. (2004, June 24). Free voluntary reading: New research, applications, and controversies. Lecture presented at PAC5 (Pan-Asian Conference). Vladivostok, Russia.

Knight, J. (2011). Unmistakable impact: A partnership approach for dramatically improving instruction. Thousand Oaks, CA: Corwin Press.

Labban, J. & Etnier, J. (2011). Effects of acute exercise on long term memory. Res Q Exercise Sport. 82: 712–721. [Pub Med]

Lee, H. (1960). *To kill a mockingbird.* New York: Harper Collins Publishers.

Levine, G. (1997) *Ella enchanted.* New York: Harper Collins Publishers.

Longhi, S. (2011). *Classroom fitness breaks to help kids focus.* New York: Scholastic.

Lowry, L. (1989). *Number the stars.* New York: Sandpiper.

Lowry, L. (1993). *The giver.* Boston: Houghton Mifflin.

Matas, C. (1993). *Daniel's story.* New York: Scholastic.

Means, B., Toyama, Y., Murphy, R., Bakia, M., & Jones, K. (2010, May). Evaluation of evidence-based practices in online learning: A meta-analysis and review of online learning studies (U.S. Department of Education, Ed.).

Meyer, C. (1992). *Where the broken heart still beats.* Orlando, FL: Harcourt.

Mitchell, M. (1936). *Gone with the wind.* New York: Macmillan Publishing Company.

More people are buying drones for fun, but they need to think of safety too. (December 14, 2014). In Newsela. Retrieved from https://newsela.com/articles/drone-popularity/id/6411/

Morris, E. (2001). *The Rise of Theodore Roosevelt.* New York: Modern Library.

Morris, E. (2010). *Colonel Roosevelt.* New York: Random House.

Nauert, R. (2008, March 12). Stress affects learning and memory. In PsychCentral. Retrieved from http://psychcentral.com/news/2008/03/12/stress-affects-learning-and-memory/2031.html.

Niemoller, M. (1995). First they came for the Jews. In Hilda Shiff (Ed.), *Holocaust poetry* (p. 9). New York: St. Martin's Press.

O'Dell, S. (1988). *Island of the blue dolphins.* New York: Sandpiper.

O'Donnell-Allen, C. (2006). *Book club connection: Literacy learning and classroom talk.* Portsmouth, NH: Heinemann.

Paratore, J. R. & Indrisano, R. (2003). Grouping for instruction in literacy. In J. Flood, D. Lapp, J. R. Squire, & J. M. Jensen (Eds.). *Handbook of research on teaching the English language arts* (2nd ed., 566–572). Mahway, NJ: Erlbaum.

Partnership for 21st Century Skills. "Framework for 21st century learning." March 2011. Web. <www.p21.org/our-work/p21-framework> 25 February 2015.

Pearson, P. D., & Gallagher, M. C. (1983). The instruction of reading comprehension. *Contemporary Educational Psychology, 8*, 317–344.

Prensky, M. (2001, October). Digital natives, digital immigrants. *On the Horizon, 9*(5), 1–6.

Promoting engagement for all students: the imperative to look within (2008). In *National Study for Student Engagement.* Retrieved from http://nsse.iub.edu/NSSE_2008_Results/docs/withhold/NSSE2008_Results_revised_11-14-2008.pdf

Rappaport, D. (2013). *To dare mighty things: The life of Theodore Roosevelt.* New York: Disney-Hyperion Books.

Ratey, J. (2008). *SPARK: The revolutionary new science of exercise and the brain.* New York: Little, Brown.

Reynolds, G. (2011, Nov. 30). How exercise benefits the brain. *The New York Times.*

Riordan, R. (2005). *The lightning thief.* New York: Miramax Books.

Rogers, K. B. (1991). The relationship of grouping practices to the education of the gifted and talented learner (RMBD91020). Storrs, CT: The National Research Center on the Gifted and Talented, University of Connecticut.

Rowlings, J. K. (1999). *Harry Potter and the sorcerer's stone.* New York: Scholastic.

Sandler, M. (2004). *Island of hope: The story of Ellis Island and the journey to America.* New York: Scholastic.

Spinelli, J. (2003). *Milkweed.* New York: Laurel-Leaf.

Taylor, M. D. (1991). *Roll of thunder, hear my cry.* New York: Puffin.

Terry, T. (2012). *Slated.* New York: Penguin Young Readers Group.

Thurber, J. (1945). *The Thurber carnival.* New York: HarperCollins Publishers.

Tutti, J., & Klein, J. (2008). Computer mediated instruction: a comparison of online and face to face. *Education technology research and development,* 56(2).

Twain, M. (2008). *The adventures of Tom Sawyer.* New York: Barnes & Noble Books.

Twain, M. (1876). *Punch brothers punch.* Retrieved from http://www.gutenberg.org/files/3184/3184-h/3184-h.htm

Wiggins, G. (2014, October 10). A veteran teacher turned coach shadows 2 students for 2 days. Retrieved from https://grantwiggins.wordpress.com/2014/10/10/a-veteran-teacher-turned-coach-shadows-2-students-for-2-days-a-sobering-lesson-learned/

Wilhelm, J. D. (2001). *Improving comprehension with think-aloud strategies.* New York: Scholastic.

Wormeli, R. (2006). *Fair isn't always equal.* Portland, ME: Stenhouse Publishers.

Yolen. J. (2004). *The devil's arithmetic.* New York: Puffin.